# THE
# INEXPLICACIONES

## Of the Dreams of Bibiana Padilla Maltos

by

## JOHN M. BENNETT

*Including*
## BIBI'S DREAMS
*by*
*Bibiana Padilla Maltos*
*and several*
*Reinexplicaciones*
*by*
*Ivan Argüelles*

/ o \
LBP
## LUNA BISONTE PRODS
2016

*Zan tontemiquico, ah nelli,*

*Ah nelli, tinemico in tlacticpac.*


*Sólo vinimos a soñar, no es cierto,*

*No es cierto, que venimos a vivir sobre la tierra.*


*We only come to dream, it's not true,*

*It's not true, that we come to live on the earth.*


*- Tochihuitzin Coyolchiuhqui*


**THE INEXPLICACIONES**
Of the Dreams of Bibiana Padilla Maltos

by John M. Bennett

Including BIBI'S DREAMS by Bibiana Padilla Maltos and several Reinexplicaciones by Ivan Argüelles

Some of these works were previously published in
Naked Sunfish/Blank Sight, Praepositiō, Otoliths;
in 2 TLPs from Luna Bisonte Prods: L'Écrit and The Entity;
and read by JMB on Psych.KG 283  - FLUX!porn / The NO!Art
Statements (one-sided LP, LTD 100)

Cover art and book design by C. Mehrl Bennett

ISBN 978-1-938521-26-3

**LUNA BISONTE PRODS**
137 Leland Ave,
Columbus, OH 43214 USA

http://www.lulu.com/spotlight/lunabisonteprods

## wiitz

the dream of a shopping cart
is your dream of a shoe
in the bottom of a lake
your dream of a book
slowly turning in a
toilet the dream of a
burning shopping cart
is the dream of a mountain
shedding its lint of
human beings the shopping
dream cart is a dream
of a forest of laundry
scattered in wind in the
wind of the shaking earth

**the dream of a tortoise is the
dream of a river running backward**

if we get
the hill o
ver la pen
umbra bursts
yr base
ment's wri
ggling cara
pace originant
ink darkened
river el
hotel del hue
so dorm ido

was the knee's
left pain the
knee's ave
nue sp read
behind tu más
cara's shell
yawning alpha
bet's sleepless
pool her thighs
her wrapper ou
verte les esca
liers her
*wheel of smoke t
urns toward you*

***Picked from the husks of
Ivan Argüelles' "anabasis xlvi"***

## the foggy mouth

the dream of hotcakes is your
dream a circular highway
described for hours a
throat a s ticky chi n
inha le the black the
b lack ex haust

*dice an form ,boil the forgotten hand*

**To make hotcakes in your dream...**
**- Bibiana Padilla Maltos**

## g utter

the dream of a ring is the
dream where you close your
mouth on a beach the
waves drown your feet w
alked b ackward from the p
arking lot sur rounded by a
fence of tires the air is limp
your hand rises toward a bird

## the inverted ground

the dream of a birth
day cake is the dream of a
tree its roots high in the
air yr head a pillow in
the center of a street a
string ties it to the tree the
wind sings its tight long arc


## the closet

the dream of the house is
the dream of rats falling off
a cliff clouds drunk with
forks the windows coughed
the dream of steps your
face turning toward the wind yr
shirt torn and bloody on the risers

## the nostril

the dream of the cake is
your dream of a watch sub
merged in the toilet water dr
ips behind the mirror your
mouth inhales a bird your
teeth crunch the bones'
leg inaction splinters
fall behind the door

## the highway reststop

your dream of feet is the
dream of fog rising from a
lake a headlight glimmers
in the weeds a hand fumbles
in a sock it means your
shoe arrived

## the circuit breaker

the dream of cancer is
your dream of the open
window your highway
potholed was your cheek
sinking in the bathrub the
ceiling light gets brighter
and brighter gets

## the orchard

the dream of apples is
your dream of laundry
knotted in the fridge
honey spreads across the
floor the sticky doorframe
smoulders was a suitcase
mildewed in the corner

## the antihistamine

the dream of nostrils is the
dream of lightbulbs in a
bowl of ground beef
muddy newspaper under the
desk your shoulders shove
through bones and empty
tissue boxes

## the book

the dream of a staircase
is the dream of a burning
sofa on the berm some
hamsters lurking in the
bushes were your slippers
clouded with fruit
flies spelling "nostril"

## the quarry

the dream of protecting
someone is the dream of
sleeping with a log or ants
chaining up the wall's your
dream of houses filled with
stones

## the bassinet

the dream of a baby is
your dream of gasoline and
underwear sprouting
flowers next a sidewalk
with a corpse across it

## the horizon

the dream of a werewolf
is the dream of a napkin
covering a cockroach be
neath your chair the dream
of sky covered with boards

## the lumber yard

the dream of a pine tree is
your dream of a toothbrush
dipped in black paint your face
with raindrops or a mask of
rotting walnuts

## the doctor

the dream of a bar is the
dream of an oily beach a
lunchbox in the glass factory
your hat soaked with blood
talking back to you

## the carpenter

the dream of a closed door
is your dream of an open door
termites swirling in a
coffee cup you drank the
air and wrote your name
on a 2 X 4

## the repast

the dream of the weather
is the dream of your
watch swirling in a colander
was the hat you wore to
strain the lunchmeat rising
to the clouds

## the journey

the dream of the rat is a
dream of a ship smoking
on the horizon where your
hand shaped the bird was
reaching for the faucet

## the portrait

the dream of fur is the
dream of a sandwich
left in a plastic bag you
kept your babyteeth in was
sweat beading on the wall

## the blister

the dream of dawn is a
dream of faucets running next
your mother returned from
France where her bladder
water stashed a dream of
magazines thrashing their
pages in a storm

## the scribe

the dream of waking up is the
dream of sleep inside your
ear a dream of rabbits
scribbling on the hood of a
car trees reflected in the
*windshield*

## the chair

the dream of waiting is the
dream of a tire deflating is
the dream of gravel in a
washing machine your
laundry sleeping in the fridge

## the face

the dream of your husband is
the dream of your wife the
dream of a window opening
and closing your eyeglasses
dusty on the sill

## evolution

the dream of animals is the
dream of time in your
wallet the dream of blankets
falling from the roof

## the turning

the dream of a hedgehog is your
dream of a shoe the
shore of the lake littered with
driftwood a dream of the
nose you hold in your hand

## the bottle

the dream of climbing a hill
is the dream of touching a
breast you swim over the
temple submerged in a
lake of milk

## the hanger

the dream of a school bus
was the dream of geese
on fire in a parking lot a
dream of trees with frozen
leaves and an ant walking in
circles walking in circles
on the sidewalk

## el tianguis

el sueño del indio es el
sueño del tepetl cabelludo
el sueño del supermercado
iluminado con leña su boca
un estanquillo es ,lleno de
luciérnagas

## the feather

the dream of a cult is
the dream of a rubber knife
in your pocket your face
hidden in a bucket a
crow explaining the
wall she sits on

## the water

the dream of a worm is the
dream of your wallet explains
the roots of shoelaces the
plot development of a bar
of soap a dream of tomatoes
bursting in rain

## la tumba

el sueño de la carretera
es un sueño de cerote
y el sueño del atl el
sueño de la flecha
verde con musgo donde
el dónde re gresa mas
nunca regresa

## the storm

the dream of a fantasy world
is not a dream but a dream of
your ledger turns to light in
the back of a closet where a
weather balloon slowly inflates

## el viaje

the dream of dirt was a
dream of nails falling
from a board a gas
station in a cloud of fog and
light surrounded by skulls
all facing in

## the wanderer

the dream of a barn is the
dream of your pants and
a cup of coffee emitting
light on the basement steps
covered with grease and
pinto bean cans a dream
of a one-way highway sign
covered with weeds

## the puzzles

the dream of your clothing
ripped is a dream of an
ocean liner crusted with
salt the dream of a broken
shovel raised in a dream of
a library where you sleep
in the reference section

## the procession

the dream of nuns was
a dream of rabbits drinking
the ink of your dream of
laundry and geese ,of steps
leading to the blood-stained
platform under the sky

## la merienda

the dream of a single nun
is the dream of being a
man in the dream of waking
in a pot of soup and
holding the fork in your hand

## el catafalco

the dream of obeying the
rules is a dream of
sleeping in a forest of
identical trees where a
single tree bursts into
flame and an ant
dreams on your forehead

## the bank

the dream of the lost dime
is the last dream of the
buried penny will stick on
your shoe the next dream
was the carseat covered with
potato chips

## the hotel

the dream of sheet music is
the dream of the mask you
couldn't wait for the dream
of a lobby filled with squeaking shoes

## the lunch

the dream of cold is the
dream of boxes under the
bed the dream of a
sandwich chattering in the
one that's under your head

**el aseo**

the dream of a jacket is
your dream of a leg on an
ironing board was the dream
of a fan sparkling in the bathtub

**the entity**

the dream of a chair was
is the dream of a kite
crashed in a tree is was
the dream of your nostril
examining your knee

**the vacation**

the dream of one necklace
will be the dream of a
cloud of nine a
dream of the beach
holding its water

**the sunflower**

the dream of a gas station
would be the dream of a
hose if your dream of a
map were the dream of
the sidewalk swallowed
in flood

**México**

the dream of the border es
el sueño del cielo el
sueño de la cama en
an earthquake es el
dream of an airplane
floating at sea

**the music**

the dream of a field will
the dream of your shoe
be the dream was itchy
is the gas station restroom
crikkking with crickets

## the murder

your dream of clothes was
the dream of a truck
parked on the berm a
dog stares at the steering
wheel will stare at the
bloody seat cover ex
haling its light

## the art gallery

the dream of a blackboard
is the dream of an alley
and a single coyote
sleeps next a fence your
face is the dream of a
mirror of a mirror and a
lipstick

## the cash

the dream of a gate is
the dream of etag a
folded in your underwear
the dream of a fountain
pen dripping with sweat

## the wrist

the dream of a window
was the dream you will
open will close your
mouth was the dream of
rain rising from a cave

## the sink

the dream of teeth is
the dream of a sidewalk
a dream of a diary
lost in the trunk of a
car your deep faucet
drips in the mirror

## the clock

the dream of your home is
the dream of laundry was the
dream of incandescent shorts
a well beneath the basement
a dream of shit and flowers

## the donuts

the dream of your coworkers
is a dream of a dream of a
field of goats eating weeds at a
fence was this the dream
of the airplane full of empty
seats?  marbles rolling and
clacking in the aisle?



## the news

the dream of a cable is a
dream of  your shoes
on the edge of a dock is the
dream of a TV smoldering
on the garage roof the sky
wrinkled ,getting dark

## media luna

the dream of a croissant
is was the dream of
the moon the dream of a
bull standing in a street a
carhorn beeping and stuck

## the bed

the dream of driving a car
could be the dream of a
rope coiled in your pants
the dream of a coin
falls off a cliff is maybe
your dream of a river
flowing into a cave

## the reflection

the dream of the color
burgundy is a dream
of your legs turning
green in a dream of a
lake covered with glass
spiders waiting on the
sur face


## the spin

the dream of an old classmate
is the dream of the back
of your head the dream
of your laundry sitting in a
pool in a dryer

**the burn**

the dream of the rock
was a dream of mist
congealing behind the
dumpsters the dumpsters
were the dream of your
eyes closing in sun


**the burn**

the dream of the rock
was a dream of mist
congealing behind the
dumpsters the dumpsters
were the dream of your
eyes closing in sun

## the flux

the dream of a hardware store
is the dream of having sex in a
bathtub is the dream of fluxus
burbling from a drain a pump
with breasts surrounded by
boxes of keys and a dream of a
shadow eating the text the text
of water dripping on the floor


## the floor

the dream of paint is a
dream of gutters full of
flies bees walking across
a roof a penis sails
over the chimney an
airplane sighs on the horizon

## the wind

the dream of a tricycle is
the dream of a hole deep
in a forest the flux of a
stream rippling with pubic hair
it's the dream of a rubber arm
clutching the air

## the truth

the dream of glitter is the
dream of a face in a crotch a
tablecloth flaps in the
breeze an instruction
manual burns in the cor
ner it's the dream of light
enclosed in a box of skin

## the fluxus leg

the dream of Mark Bloch is
a dream of a warehouse of
blank books a lens
hangs from the ceiling it's
a dream of a rabbit standing
on hind legs in a bedroom
thronged with naked women

## the diver

the dream of facebook is
the dream of a silent
room with semen stained
walls the dream of a
pickup truck parked behind a
dumpster

## the mildew

the dream of an invitation is
a dream of faucets opened
in a basement a bed
heaped with underwear a
windowshade punctured with
tiny holes

## the lingering

the dream of losing a friend
is the dream of a doorbell
ringing late at night the
dream of a passionate kiss
at the base of your spine it's
the dream's opening a fridge
and reaching for the hairless cat

## the subway

the dream of New York City
is the dream of your foot
being sucked by an
enormous man naked in a
bowler hat and the dream
of an ant suspended in air

## the porch

the dream of Keith Buchholz is a
dream of whispers in the
laundromat a dragonfly
landing on your tongue ton
gue's a curtain undulating
in *a a bbreeze swirling
around the TV screen*

## la merienda

the dream of your home is the
dream of carrots in the
trunk of a car a tire
leans on a fire hydrant tu
mano abierta en el horno
lleno de cohetes en tu boca
un cerillo

## the sidewalk

the dream of Allen Bukoff was
the dream of a bed without
mattress the frame glistened
with motor oil and your
face was a blanket doll
prickly with seeds

**the letter**

the dream of C. Mehrl & John M. Bennett
is a dream of flashlights sinking
in the sea a ship sails back
ward drawkcab speaking
through the faucet falls
from your mouth
coughing in the
clouds deep
in a cave

**the mirror**

the dream of your friend could
be a dream of a pencil
writing the dream of your
friend could be the
dream of a pen or sill
eaten by termites' a
dream of your friend
eating a pencil

**the clouds**

the dream of a circle is the
dream of a corner of a
bedroom the dream of a
cricket lurks by the
sausage sweating on
your plate's a dream
of a doorbell clanging
in your pocket's a
circular dream a maerd
elcric elcric maerd




**the lawn**

the dream of going to work
in  the nude is a dream
of a phonebook a dream
of a canvas tarp and a
dream of layered red
worms in a compost
heap it's the dream of a
cookie crumbling in your lap

## the tissue

the dream of sleep is the
sleep of dream is the
dream of toenails
lifted from their beds is
the dream of peels and
senots the dream of maerd
swirling in a golden bowl

## the ringtone

the dream of your friend
cheating on her spouse is
a dream of mothballs
breathing in a closet is
a dream of fog in the
kitchen cabinets and a
dream of your friend
cheating on his spouse

## the storm

the dream of a festive banquet
was the dream of a ceiling
dripping blood is the dream
of ducks drowned in a
sea of wine the
dream of a marble
rolling far beneath the bed

## the degree

the dream of a chair is
maybe a dream of a
beach streaked with
oil the dream of a
handkerchief stuffed in
your mouth the dream
of a poem you wipe your
ass with

## the test

the dream of an audience was
the dream of a shoe
stored in a freezer the
freezing a dream of your
fork lost in a fork a
dream of tequila and a
moth drying in your mouth
drying in your mouth
which never closes

## the seeming

the dream of the dog is the
dream of a river behind the
door the door a dream of
wind buffeting your
face dream of a
cow chewing in the
streambed's your dream
of a neck turned over's
your waiting sleep is
the dream of everything
is more than it is

## the whistle

the lunch in your foot is
the stone curled in your
pocket is the fog
posted before your door
is the back of a letter
you mailed returned
last week is the sun
burning in a tree

## the cup

the fork in your pants
was the cake mouldering
in the trunk of your car
is the faucet named for a
snake was the lightswitch
crawling toward the floor the
floor is your typewriter
forgetting its lines

## the trowel

the dream of a key is the
dream of a glass of milk
leaking into the mattress the
dream of trees whipping in
wind the wind a dream
of laundry with meat
in the pockets

## the fragrant window

the dream of a nocturnal visitor
is the dream of your visitation
of the used car lot the dream
of coins clinking in your pocket
your knees suddenly stiff and
burning a beard left on the
dining room table

## the parking lot

the dream of a warehouse is a
dream of an empty beach the
dream of an SUV parked
in your living room the
room a dream of your
mouth with rows of rusty teeth

## the green path

the dream of seeing a doctor is
the dream of an empty picture
frame the frame contains your
face your face a finger raised
to your ear your ear a dream of
Tlaloc sucking a mossy stone

## the dental floss

the dream of a gate was a
dream of a red glass heart
beneath your shirt your
shirted meatloaf the
dream of air you entered
air you enter leave behind

## the towel

the dream of your sister is a
dream of a hole in a tree a
dream of needles rusting in a
box is a dream of napkins
floating on a lake your dream
forgot

## the mother

the dream of a towel is the
dream your lake forgot the
dream of napkins floating
in a box of rusting pins the
dream of a hollow tree
where your sister sleeps

## the laundry

the dream of your mother is
the dream of cream cheese
softened in your hair your
hairs a dream of flies
still against a window
where your dream re
turns the other dream's
your mother

## the rest stop

the dream of a bench is a
dream of the dream in a
car going 80 MPH under a
bridge the bridge was
dream of water fills
your mouth of water
boiling in the fridge

## the book drop

the dream of a library is the
dream of a shirt filled with
sandwich meat the meat your
dream of waking in a camera
the dream of stairs circling a
coffin and a coffin in your
dream the cup of coffee
you read and drop in a toilet

## the sawmill

the dream in an art gallery
could be the dream of
shoes left in the garden
the dream of foghorns
gurgling in rain
must be a dream of a
warehouse a warehouse
filled with toilet paper
filled with birds blinking bl
inking tiny bright eyes




## the thirst

the dream of a dream of a
coffee shop is the
dream of a sidewalk leaving
the dream of a nickel dreams
of 20 pesos y una puente
sobre el río seco
repleto de cadáveres

## the dismembered

the dream of remembering the
dream you dreamed tomorrow
was the dream you folded
into a cootie catcher the
dream you will forgot today
the dream of lymph nodes
swoll with fluid you dream
you will remember forgot
the dream you never will re
membered

## la peluca

the dream of being depressed
will be just a dream of
counting change the
dream of combing hair
before a mirror invisible
dream of dream of
folding a mask and
eating the ants fall out

## the frame

the dream of your clothes is
the same dream of your clothes
the dream of water running
down walls was the same dream
of water running down glass is
the dream of a lawn in twilight is
not the dream of lawn in twilight
but the dream of a twilit lawn a
large red ball under a tree

## the burden

the dream of a bathroom was
the dream of a telephone is
the dream of mud drying on
the back seat floor was the
dream of a king buried
deep beneath a temple

## the leg

the dream of glass was the
dream of shadows in the
glass the dream of a fork
dropped beneath your chair
the dream was a glass of
milk with a toy car inside the
glass of milk was not the
dream of glass it was the
dream of glass

## the fence

the dream of a construction site
might be the dream of wind
crossing a lake might be the
dream of a tree shiny with
ice or might be the dream
of a construction site high
on a hill under the stars

## the blade

the dream of the question is
your question of the dream
was the guess you didn't
know was the dream you
warbled at your sandwich
was the questioned meat
your dream recalled the
questionnaire you threw in the fire

## the sausage

the dream of a lobby is
a dream of your shoes is
the dream of a cigarette
floating in a cup of
coffee is the dream of a
roof covered with sleeping
women the dream of
stairs rising through the
doors to the street

## the nodding

the dream of the bookstore
is the dream of your hat
full of kleenex is the dream
of having to take a dump's a
dream of silence which is the
dream of muzak soaked into
pages of a book the dream
of a bookstore was the dream of
bratwurst drying in the sun

## the predicate

the dream of a bookshelf is
the dream of a window the
dream of dirt on the
window is the dream of
knowing what will never
happen is the dream of
flies walking on paper

## the shudder

the dream of warmth in a
dream is the dream of
warmth in the fridge in
the fridge you touch the
sweaty head the head
was frigid covered with
parsley the dream of
parsley's the dream of
hair you were eating in
the warmth of dream

## the lint

the dream of a movie is the
movie of a dream is the dream
of a sidewalk in the opposite
direction is the dream of a
sidewalk moving  into the
sidewalk's dream of a
fountain spraying milk a
tiny boat sinking at the edge

**the supper**

the dream of death is the
dream holding a hammer the
dream of lung caged in a
circus is a dream of frogs
asleep on the ceiling where
your wooden hand reaches
air oil fills your glasses case the
dream you dead's a dream a
garden planted with forks



**R**

d
dr
dre
drea
drea*nm*M**or** *n*

## the gift

the dream of a desk is a
dream of a grave beneath
your feet the dream of
broken crockery rattling
in a box you tied with a
bow is the dream of
bones and charcoal in a
drawer you opened and
bang your knee against

## the road

the dream of a wheelchair is
a dream of chalk faces drawn
on the driveway the dream of a
TV facing the wallpaper where a
soap opera flickers was the dream
of a ladder raised against the sky

## the altar

the dream of hay in a
corner of your house is
the dream of books and
mail stored in the basement
the basement a dream of
school with oatmeal spilled
on the floor your dream of
laundry fluttering in a church

## the glottis

the dream of books hung
out like laundry is the dream
of Ginny Lloyd reading *2666*
de Roberto Bolaño is the dream
of a mountain quivering against
the sky the sky was the dream of
a ladder flickering in a TV screen

**the flies**

the dream of a photo is the
dream of a window screen
covered with ants with ants
covering a dream of coins
falling from the sun the sun
a dream of paperweights
pressed against your eyes


**the stool**

the dream of your dream not
making sense was a dream of
mountains in the rear view
mirror was the maerd rorrim
falling into your next dream
is the dream of a pool of milk
where you dream of waking in
the former dream formed of
stones on a road where there
are no cars

## el tocino

el sueño del asiento del coche
es el sueño de un par de huevos
rancheros es el sueño de una
familia que no sea tuya pero
parece ser la tuya en un siglo
venidero es un sueño de
equipaje de una maleta con
un par de huevos divorciados
que se juntan con sus salsas en
tu mano que cae del timón
y se duerme

## el reloj

el sueño de un restaurante es
un sueño de cocodrilos dormidos
en el fondo del río el sueño de tus
guantes perdidos en la lluvia de
la lluvia que es el sueño del sol
acostado en las fauces de un
alcalde muerto que es el sueño
del sueño de una pluma dormida
en el despertar del ganso

## the seep

el sueño de la puerta es el
sueño de la piscina donde nada
un bisonte flaco es el sueño
de la lluvia del puerto de
barcas hundidas ,hundidas
con cabelleras llenas de lodo


## la cesta

el sueño de la tortilla es
un sueño de la mano que
se abre con piedra insomne
el sueño del olor de tu cabeza
es el sueño soñado de la
toalla mojada de humo

## el licántropo

el sueño del hotel es el
sueño del calzado que al
canza el fango al otro
lado del mar es el sueño
del bolsillo lleno de grillos
que cantan al unísono y
el sueño de una cama mo
jada en el avión


## el sudor

el sueño de tu cara es
cultórica es el sueño
insoñado de la grava
alrededor de tu cuña es
el sueño de una es
tátua vestida de hojas
en el sótano de la
casa de tus abuelos de
tus tatarabuelos que ha
blan con bocas de agua

## les flics

un sueño de la tragaluz
es un sueño del enjambre
de bocas es el sueño de
la oscuridad que sueña
en la cara del sol o en
el foco que se estrella
en las ondas de tu habla
que habla con dientes de
cristal y gárgaras de
lago disecado

## el zopilote

el sueño del pico que te
sale de la boca es el
sueño de un cuarto de
huéspedes en una casa
suburbana es el sueño
de arúgula ahogada en
aceite y de un motor
de coche enterrado
en el traspatio con los
huesos de un perro amarillo

## las mesas

el sueño de una cámara
es el sueño de una cámara
de arena es el sueño de
una cámara inflada como
globo es el sueño de una
cámara utilizada como
guante y el sueño de una
cámara que es el sueño
de un guante del sueño es
una cámara o anu aramác
escondida en tu gorra arrog
ut ne adidnocse

## el sueño

el sueño del café es el
sueño de la arena in
visible de tu ojo izquierdo
el sueño del derecho es u
n agujero en el cristal de
la ventana con vista de
la sierra y se cierra con
un pañuelo empapado de
orinas

## the sortage

the dream of your back yard is the
dream of your back you walk back
on the pure shoe's a dream of an
empty shower where you spell your
knife you spell N I F E the *K* rat
tling in a bush your dream of
termites is a dream laughing
in a bloody hospital gown

## the jewels

the dream of a refrigerator is the
dream of a vase of flowers flow
ers the dream of a rusty can of
beans the dream of the vomitator
giggling on the back porch where
you dreamed a porch under
water from the flood your
corn flakes sink in

## el equipaje

the dream of concrete blocks
was the dream of the is your
kleenex folded on the table
is the soggy hole in your
shorts buried in the garden
was and is a dream of Pluto
clucking in the cargo hold a
plane falls to the horizonte
el horizonte donde el mar se olvida

## the correction

the dream of your arms around a
neighbor is the dream of your arms
in the sky the sky a dream of your
haircut disappears in a cloud
your dream of the dream of a
sidewalk covered with ants a
dream of the shiny things
move past your feet in the night

## the shut

the dream of a sleeping pill is
the dream of a child reading a
wooden ruler dreams of a wind
ow dreams of a window's
feather laid on your eye's the
dream of a fork with tines on
each end a broken glass
beneath the table

## the siege

the dream of anger is the
dream of an empty path
across the puna the dream
of mountains' closed eyes
swaying on the horizon it's
it's the dream of your chest
covered with gnats and your
breasts flowering next a
stream it's the dream of a
chair smiling and
faced the corner

## el mesquite

the dream of a teacher is a
dream of a stinky deck of
cards the dream of cookies c
rushed in your hat is the
dream of a piscina shim
mering in a Chihuahua
desert highway curves
toward distant hill is the
dream of a pencil scribbling
on the back of your hand

## la fiesta

the dream of a bicycle is the
dream of an ear of corn sh
ucked and stuck in the s
pokes' a dream of a mouth
speaking its teeth is the
dream of a summer dress
waving in the wind
high on a pole

## lo oscuro

the dream of a forest of equipales
was a dream of a muddy pool the
pool a dream of an equipal f
alling apart on a roof the roof
a dream of a foot and a
bar of soap the soap a
dream of bicycles streaming
off a cliff was the dream of a
forest of equipales

## the shout

the dream of pajamas is
the dream of cows is
the dream of language is
the dream of a ladder is
the dream of a cave is
the dream of your hand is
the dream of a sausage
turning in the shoe
beneath your bed

## the novel

the dream of transparent
shorts is the dream of a
hand covering your ear the
dream of an asshole
stuffed with paper where a
tale of the transparent shorts
was explained and denied it
was the dream of a pane of
glass folded and stapled
in the bottom drawer

## the mold

the dream of the barefoot
lobster is the dream of a
spoon thrown from the
boat the dream of a
corn flake stuck in your
beard the dream of
your beard is the
dream of being a woman
which is the dream of being a
woman when you wake up as a
woman on a slippery deck

## the leap

the dream of being in a movie
is the movie of being in a
dream is the dream of
a chair stuck to the
ceiling is the dream of
a basement full of
leaking canned peas the
dream of a broom
walking up the stairs

## the whirlpool

the dream of popcorn is the
dream of toilet paper
swelling in your mouth was
the dream of a dog circling
the ladder is the dream
of laundry or the dream of
laundry is the dream of
sleeping in the kitchen
without clothes

## the issue

the dream of a floor is the
dream of your broken arm
is the dream of a washer cl
anking in your pocket was
the dream of a green stone
glued to your tongue was
the dream of the spinal
speech that would tell the
name of the dream of the
floor was the dream of the wall

## the towel

the dream of cramps is the
dream of fishing line st
retched across the water is
the dream of a sandwich
drying in the bottom of a
fridge it's your mouth
open but closed closed
but open as you face the door

## la frontera

the dream of a shower is the
dream of a desert with a
fence running through it the
dream of stones in the
shadow of mesquite
it's the dream of thunder
heard in the attic where
bees slowly circle

## l'écrit

the dream of blood is the
dream of chicken soup and a
bowl of muddy crackers it's
the dream of a nostril and a
dream of a rope it's the
dream of diarrhea a
cup of coffee steaming
next the bed where it's
the dream of blood
the dream of fountain pens

## the gauge

the dream of the motorcycle
is the dream of a dreamed
flea asleep in your shoe
is the dream of your eyelid
torn from your face was
the dream of watches
stored in a rusty bucket

## the chain

the dream of the kiss was
the dream of the ssik the
dream of the faucet the
tecuaf and the dream of
the leg you soothed with
gel it's the dream of a
market filled with pots
,pitahayas ,ladders

## la tumba

the dream of the bouncy-house
is the dream of a hill
with a pyramid inside it's
the dream of a tree`
covered with naranja agria
y es el sueño de
una ventana con espejos
en lugar de cristales

## the bulb

the dream of a garage is
the dream of sleep when
you dream of cans of
olive oil and wind in the
trees the dream of the
garage is a dream of
screwdrivers soaking
in the sink is the
dream of a book its
pages rustling in wind

## the rinse

the dream of night is the
dream of dawn rising in
your underwear is the
dream of a tent
where you stored your
hat collection it's the
dream of the flapping
of an invisible flag

## the chew

the dream of searching for
something is the dream of a
neck on the pillow next to
you in bed is the dream
of a garbage bag tightly
sealed against gnats it's
the dream of a foghorn a
dream of a ladder
falling from a dock

## the swelling

the dream of a curb is the
dream of your knuckle in
pain as you grip the pen is
the dream of rain falling
across the street is the
dream of standing in the
sunlight with water
streaming down your face

## the cheese

the dream of your daughter
was the dream of a
restaurant where you sit
at a table again and a
gain the dream of a
lawn closely mowed
with something emerging
from under the dream
of a ham sandwich
covered with a wig
calling your name

## the sun

the dream of being almost
hit by a car is the dream
of a wooden box filled
with knives or the dream
of a shoe made of meat or
a dream of frogs a dream
of wind a dream of la
undry t umbling dow n st airs


## the itch

the dream of roast chi
cken breasts is the dream
of a garbage can shining in
the sun is the dream of a
sidewalk covered in green
leaves the dream of eggs
rolling down a hill into the
hands of squirrels

## the scab

the dream of raw chicken
was the dream of your
hands running through your
hair the hair was the dream
of paper bags filled with
wind is the dream of a
sidewalk covered with water

## the churn

the dream of chickens hiding
behind your door is the
dream of a well brimming
with feathers feathers
could be the dream of smoke
in your lungs was the speech
you never gave because the
lights wouldn't turn off
was the dream of a rowboat
swaying in a tree

## the pool

the dream of breasts is the
dream of never dying it's
the dream of a storm br
eaking the plates in the
basement the dream of
stairs rising into
blinding light and the
dream of sleep in your
dream from which you
wake but never wake

## los lentes

the dream of broccoli is the
dream of your mother
holding a twin is the dream
of a bowl you wear on
your head was the dream
of eyeglasses hidden beneath
the bed where something
invisible is mumbling
verses in your sleep

## el ápice

el sueño de la lechuga es el
sueño del vaso de leche
es el sueño soñado del
viento circular con la
máscara de Xiuhtecuhtli
en el centro del sueño
donde hay una torta de
jamón y el dedo índice
de la estatua del sueño


## the shoulder

the dream of green fields is
the dream of your pants whirling
in the washer the dream
of your tired arm resting
on a tire it was is the
dream of a dog asleep
in the trunk of a car

## the sore

the dream of plastic wrap
was the dream of a
cardboard box full of
sand the sand was the
dream of your eye the
eye was the dream of your
leg the leg the dream of
a shadow tightly sealed
with plastic wrap

## the town

the dream of the Brillo pad
art competition was the
dream of a forest or the
dream of a room filled with
your shirts it will be the
dream you had last year of a
face covered with burning
hair and the dream of a gas
station with dirty rutted
snow where a car is
spspinningng itts whwheels

*Inexplicación of JMB's dream*

## the town

the dream of the Brillo pad
art competition was the
dream of a forest or the
dream of a room filled with
your shirts it will be the
dream you had last year of a
face covered with burning
hair and the dream of a gas
station with dirty rutted
snow where a car is
spspinningng itts whwheels

*Inexplicación of JMB's dream*

## the sherds

the dream of plastic wrap is
the dream of your hand held
up to the sun is the dream
of a hole in the sky full
of tepalcates tepalcates
the dream of your cup of
coffee slowly floating
through the window
to the empty street

## las obras completas

the dream of being on a roof
is the dream of bees
circling the chimney
is the dream of
sky filled with
water the water the
dream of my face be
neath your face which
is the face of Augusto Monterroso

## the tongue

the dream of a gin martini
is the dream of an olive
tree in Andalucía is the
dream of a table in an
airport restroom where
a woman sits and counts
her fingers it's the dream
of a gun hidden beneath
the water heater and a door
opening into a brightly lit hall

## el éxtasis

el sueño de la pregunta es
el sueño de escribir esta
inexplicación que es el
sueño de una apertura en
la pared de la cocina donde hay
una cabeza que te pregunta
lo que hay dentro de la pared
que es el sueño de la inex
plicación escrita mas no escrita

## the spokes

the dream of the parking garage
is the dream of a waiter
sleeping in a shower stall it's
the dream of a tunnel at the
center of time with roads
leading up to the light in all
directions the dream of the
light is the dream of a tire
spinning above your head

## the bankrupt

the dream of your partner
leaving you is the dream
of a shirt rotting behind
the toilet is the dream
of a ladder with broken
rungs it's the dream of
hair without a face and the
dream of scissors
walking across the floor

## the sandwich

the dream of the jacket you
wore in the rain is the
dream of your hand
touching your face is the
dream of an itchy wart
on your nose and the
dream of your armpit
cuddling a worm it's
the dream of fog lif
ting as the sun comes up

## the singer

the dream of smoking in
the dream of a river
running through trees
is the dream of a fork
dividing the wind and the
dream of hanging upside
down from the ceiling


## the swim

the dream of the leftover
egg salad sandwich was the
dream of a chicken lost in a
forest the dream of a
tongueless shoe coughing
up feathers the feathers a
dream of wet coins sliding
around in your pocket

## the song

the dream of the dress and
high heels is the dream
of a door whose glass is
covered with spit a
man in a blanket sleeps
at the base it's the dream
of a zipper folded across
the sky and the dream of a
ladle drying under a tree

## the nodder

the dream of gunpowder is the
dream of an archaeological dig
in a hole full of pencils it's a
dream of the wind itching
in a bottle the bottle
shining on the highest shelf
next a gun dripping oil or
coca cola

## la tierra

el sueño de tu casa en la
Avenida Reforma es el
sueño del túnel por los
huesos del lago es el
sueño del cielo escrito
con humo y es el sueño
de una choza invertida
en el monte de chapulines
con murallas de agua

## el ala

el sueño de los pájaros es
un sueño de toneladas de
madera la madera el sueño
de pajaracos que son el
sueño de árboles caídos
los árboles caídos son el
sueño de un zopilote que
se dormita en tu recámara
con la madera mojada
de tus sueños

## la cumbre

el sueño de una camada de
gatos es el sueño de la
escalera que sube al techo
el sueño del techo es el
sueño del libro que se
bosteza en el baño os
curo que es el sueño
de las garras que te
acarician las piernas

## el tornasol

el sueño del jacuzzi es un
sueño de polvo enlatado
en tu bodega y es el sueño
del jacuzzi invisible debajo
de tu peluca la peluca
es un sueño del sueño que
es el sueño del amanecer
rosado en el sótano

## la muerte

el sueño de hablar por
celular es el sueño
de respirar por una
sábana de hule que
es un sueño de abrir
los ojos y verlos
cerrados es el sueño
de la luna tinta como
vino y el sueño de los
dientes que se cierran en
el tallo de una cempoalxochitl


## el dolor

el sueño de hablar muchísimo
es el sueño del río que cae
en una caverna es el
sueño de la chachalaca que
se calla como túmulo de
tortugas que son el sueño
de la indagación de los
factores fiscales del
intercambio respiratorio
entre las clases económicas

## la carretera

el sueño de los Paipais es
el sueño del alambrado es
piral que te cerca mas no
te cerca es el sueño de la
ramada que cubre la
ausencia de una estátua
y es el sueño de la estátua
que se come el alambre

## el tomar

the dream of a glass dis
play case is the dream
of a knife falling to the
floor is the dream of your
leg stuck to the ceiling it's
the dream of a tuna sandwich
y el sueño de tunas bajo el
sol del mediodía es el
sueño de bostezar con la
boca llena de agua

## the tub

el sueño del baño fué el
sueño de volver al super
mercado que fue el sueño
de mirar la basura a flote
en el superficie del cenote
was the dream of an ear
of corn stuck in your
anus like light

## the use

the dream of a pedestal is
the dream of a spoon stuck
in the earth and the
dream of your arm
reaching for fog
reaching for fog
that climbs to the ceiling

## the shovel

the dream of a family reunion
is the dream of grass covered
with cups is the dream of
milk spilled on a tree trunk
it's the dream of roots
shriveling like worms in
the roof of a tool shed
slowly slumping into the
canal at the end of your back yard

## the cathair

the dream of the map is the
dream of your face
skinned like a peach
was the dream of an
outhouse falling off a
cliff or was it a
dream of the wires
knotted and dusty
under your desk?

**the shadow**

the dream of Luc Fierens
was the dream of padlocks
falling from a passenger
plane was the dream of
birds made of cathair
waiting at the door which
was the dream of a
swimming pool splashing
with cardboard fish

**the ask**

the second dream of
Allen Bukoff was the dream
of maggots knocking on the
front door which was the
dream of clawing on the
back door which was the
dream of rain pouring
down the chimney and
puddling like mercury in
front of the bookcase

## the knob

the dream of the coordinating
committee is the dream
of a table made of string
the dream of string was
the dream of your lunch
a rancid sandwich
of political correctness was
the dream of walking out
the door onto a sidewalk
covered with glittering ants

## the wish

the dream of sleeping is the
dream of waking the dream
of waking is the dream
of sleeping in a bathtub the
dream of the bathtub is the
dream of waking in a
mask the dream of the
mask is the dream of
being asleep as the
tsunami arrives

## the transmission

the dream of driving a car
was the dream of a bag of
bricks bursting its contents
down the stairs it's the
dream of buying a flexible
ladder which is the
dream of a tire in a
pillowcase under your head

## la cerradura

el sueño de la computadora
es el sueño de un vacío
en tu frente el vacío el
sueño de un ojo que ve al
revés y el ojo el sueño
de una pantalla de piedra
donde corre un hilo de sangre

## el huayno

el sueño del huésped es
el sueño de la pared de
agua la pared el sueño
de una silla en llamas
y las llamas el sueño
de la puna cubierta
de enormes bloques de hielo


## el roto

el sueño del libro es el
sueño de la almohada es
crita de tu cara es el
sueño del coche sin llantas
desaparecido cuando aman
ece la noche es el sueño de
los calzoncillos invisibles
que te llevas al soñar

## la luna

el sueño del plumón amarillo
es el sueño de tu boca a
bierta en el comedor el
comedor es el sueño soñado
del trueno que te rodea
la cabeza y tu cabeza
el sueño de tu fin en
la caverna de los antepasados


## el cálculo

el sueño del control es el
sueño de tu mano biónica
es el sueño de una cobija
mojada de orinas y el
sueño de una ventana
cegada con moscas que
son el sueño de 2 mas 1
que no son 3

## el techo

el sueño del péndulo
meditado es el sueño
del viento arenoso que
sopla por las mangas
de tu camisa que es el
sueño del manual incom
prensible del televisor
que es el sueño de la
nada que no es la nada

## la laminación

el sueño del letrero es un
sueño del encendedor que
es el sueño del grillo que
te habla en su lengkikua es
el sueño del foco negro
en la caja debajo de tu
cama donde sueñas con un
letrero carbonizado que
protesta los asesinatos
de estudiantes

## el manjar

el sueño de estar interruptido
es el sueño de seguir con el
betunazo de tus zapatos
es el sueño del corredor
de un hospital de cancerosos
y es el sueño de una
cura por medio de chiles
serranos y chiltepequines

## el libro

el sueño del líquido corrector es el
sueño de tomar lo blanco como
blanco de tu vista es el
sueño del tren que sale del
túnel que es el sueño de un
texto intestino que te
abre las tripas y te
revela el secreto

## sueño soñado

el sueño de la luna es
el sueño de vino tinto
que por si mismo habla
por el sueño del celular
para los dientes perdidos
en el sueño del axolotl
que mira sin ojos
hacia la arena que es
el sueño que muere
dentro la luna en su aire
sin historia soñando
un desierto de mercurio
siempre pero siempre
en otro sueño del laberinto
de todos los sueños
que circulan en el polvo
del espacio sin fin


*Ivan Argüelles soñando con John M. Bennett*

## the screen

the dream of the class re
union is the dream of feet
walking up a wall the wall
a dream of leaves swirling
in wind the wind is a
dream of hair c
c overing a swimming pool


## the olive

the dream of a martini
was the dream of a thick
fog on your porch the
door stands open and a
white russian mumbles to
you in your sleep which is
the dream of waking up
holding a glass in each hand

## el asesino

the dream of a chair is
the dream of a fire in a
garbage can it's the
dream of your legs
opening a ladder which
is the dream of a well
overflowing with blood

## the sleep

the dream of being tired was
maybe the dream of a bird
was maybe the dream of
an ant dreaming on the
ceiling was maybe the
dream of corn stalks
bending in wind

## el peregrinaje

the dream of walking in a
desert es el sueño de
encontrar una taza rota
is the dream of a tree
with a shiny car in its
branches es el sueño
de un pozo de agua
en tu calavera enterrada
la calavera es un dream of a k
nife hidden under your mattress

## the ceiling

the dream of floating on
water is the dream of
a stone carried in your
pocket for years is
the dream of a mattress sw
arming with fiddler crabs the
crabs are a dream of your
hands held up to the light

## the squirrels

the dream of an oasis is
the dream of a painting on
the wall of a motel room
the motel a dream of your
underpants soaking in a
bathtub full of motor oil
it's the dream of a
comic book open on
the table where a TV hums


## the spoon

the dream of the floor is
the dream of a rabbit
drowned in a cenote
the cenote a dream of an
opening eye in a sausage
factory where the floor
is covered with plastic
tape dispensers

## the loaf

the dream of wearing pants is
the dream of mosquitos asleep
under the garden's leaves
the leaves the dream of of
yyour ttongue ttasting a
window it's the dream of a
sandwich filled with
ham and plastic bags

## la cumbre

the dream of your grandparents
is the dream of a grasshopper
waiting in the fridge es el sueño
del agua que te espera en las
paredes y es el sueño del taxi
que te llevará a la frontera
donde te espera una flauta

## the singe

the dream of cleaning your room
is the dream of a faucet
mounted on the wall is the
dream of your face looking
in at itself it's the dream of a
sidewalk where a line of
dogs is sitting
facing your house




## the clue

the dream of a box es el
sueño del agua ,a fin de
cuentas ,todos los sueños
son sueños del agua ,is the
dream of a brush held
up to the sun and the
dream of rain which is
not the dream of rain

## the plunger

the dream of mice is the
dream of *the* is the dream
of ice cubes nested on your
pillow it's the dream of a
television smoking in the
bathroom is the dream of a
football covered with mildew

## the swell

the dream of fur was
the dream of sand in
your shoes is the dream
of needles falling from a
tree was the dream of a
boat being driven toward
rocks is the dream of your
hand caressing your butt

## la sarna

the dream of the devil is
the dream of a politician
demanding the end of time was
the dream of a mask grinning
in a mirror is the dream of
corndogs boiling in oil was
the dream of your mouth
abierta y salivante por comer

## the crisp

the dream of eating eggs
would be the dream of
your lap if the dream of
your lap were the dream
of a cancer eating your
cheek if the dream of
your cheek were the
dream of a window shade
flapping up to reveal the sun

## el ché

el sueño de estirarse es el
sueño de tu lengua donde
está escrito *nombre* es
el sueño del acento argentino
de una yegua blanca que
te espera en la esquina
con un discurso sobre
las piedras verdes del monte

## el templo

el sueño de ser coreógrafo
es el sueño de ser coreógrafa
que es el sueño de un par
de cucharones que son
el sueño de la sombra
en la gaveta de tu abuela
la abuela que es el
sueño del amanecer con
cohetes en Chichicastenango

## el congrio

el sueño de la pistola es el
sueño de la lluvia el
sueño de la lluvia es el
sueño del punto final de
tu memorial al fiscal el
sueño de la memoria es el
sueño de un lago donde
se duerme la pistola
con su amor la anguila

## el principio

el sueño de la acera es
el sueño del pasto que se
extiende al horizonte es
un sueño del círculo que
forman tus ojos con el
mundo y el sueño del mundo
es el sueño de la nada como
torre que desaparece en el cielo azul

## el lúmen

el sueño de estar perseguido
no es el sueño del sendero
el sendero no es el sueño
de la choza de vidrio la
choza no es el sueño del
túnel que no es el sueño
del mar y el mar no es
el sueño de huir por las
llamas del incendio en el bosque


## el cerillo

el sueño del insulto que te
echan no es el sueño de
una diente en la tina
sino el sueño de una
esquina con estanquillo
donde se vende sólo
dedos cercenados y es
el sueño de un ojo
que se abre en el cielo
con una sonrisa de nube

## el correr

el sueño del poni ¿era
un sueño de cucarachas?
¿de pepinos era el sueño
de las cucarachas? ¿los
pepinos el sueño de
la cumbre del picchu eran
,donde te espera una
piedra barbuda? ¿no es
el sueño de tu gorra
perdida por el río?

## el frío

el sueño de la cabra
con un abrigo de hule
puede ser el sueño
de una cabeza de níquel
o el sueño de una zorra
que toma leche mas no
puede ser, no puede ser el
sueño de un abrigo con la
cabeza niquelada de una
zorra que te habla de tu
mamá con su bolso de hojas

## eye of the bowl

the dream of trying to pee
is the dream of tearing a
yellow shirt the yellow
skirt the dream of
red coins falling on the
table the cable rises
folds you in an abrazo
un embarazo de orinas y
papas fritas de sapos fritos
y es el sueño de un coche
con las ventanas cerradas

## the grease

the dream of a maid cleaning
your house is the dream of a
hole in the roof your hair
flies through the dream of
your hair is the dream of a
bowl of linguini and sausage
the dream of linguini is the
dream of your tongue split
into grass bending in wind

## la encuadernación

el sueño de leer una nota es
el sueño del aceite que te
llena el zapato derecho
que es el sueño del izquierdo
que es una novela en trizas
que son el sueño de tu
cabellera rizada donde se
anida un gorrión o una cicada

## la cartera

el sueño de ver unos dólares
es el sueño del dolor del
hígado mas no es el sueño
del alambre telefónico sino
el sueño del alambrado
fronterizo que es el sueño de
tus dientes apretados en un
ladrillo mas no el sueño de
tu nombre escrito con
dentifricio en el espejo

## the colander

the dream of instructions is
the dream of a book burning
in the corner a book falling
off a cliff to the sea the sea is
the dream of instructions you
don't understand and the dream
of a face and a bee asleep in your hat


## las plumas

el sueño de comer pollo fué
el sueño de la caca pintada
en la pared la pared el sueño
de pollo frito con sardinas y
piedras verdes las piedras
verdes no eran el sueño del
pollo comido sino el sueño
del pollo hablador que te h
ace acordar de las hojas secas
que te cubren las mejillas

## the nails

the dream of medicine is a dream
of towels afloat in a river it's
the dream of padlocks covered with
oil which is a dream of a one-eyed
owl crawling under the bed where
you dream of bullets and empty
cartons of toilet paper

## el sordo

el sueño de una casa con
muchas habitaciones es el
sueño de un solo cuarto el
sueño del cuarto es el sueño
de una regla sin números los
números ausentes son el
sueño de escaleras y escaleras
donde te esperan unos
gallos callados

## el túnel

el sueño de pasar por la
puerta no puede ser el
sueño del aire pero sí es
el sueño del airado que
te sopla una receta para
frijoles con huevos los
huevos son el sueño
proyectil de un escupitazo
que se esfuma por la
puerta de luz


## the chowder

the dream of blueberries is the
dream of your eyes floating
in a cup of coffee it's the
dream of your brain filled
with purple ink and the dream
of a faucet leaking slowly
in your pants

## la mercancía

the dream of asking the price
is the dream of the
broken mask in your
pocket your pocket's
the dream of ash in
your hands which are
the dream of fish
circling your thighs
as you count the
coin in your mouth

## the issues

el sueño del vestido es el
sueño de la bandera fu
turista the bandera
is the dream of a foot spl
ashing in the toilet bowl
que es el sueño de
esperar bajo un árbol el
taxi que llega and honks
like a goose

## the sea

the dream of the office is the
dream of crumbled crackers
falling from the ceiling the
ceiling the dream of the fog
thick under your blank
ets  .but the blankets are
not the dream of entering
the highway at dusk with
no other cars on the road

## the crowd

the dream of your coworkers
is the dream of a broken
chair was the dream of a
closet full of wigs is the
dream of a shining fount
ain in the basement was
the dream of a fork
singing your name


## the itches

the dream of christmas is the
dream of a sweaty sandwich
in the bottom of the fridge
it's the dream of a broken
window filled with light
and the dream of a log
rolling down a hill
coming to rest in
a parking lot

## the choice

the dream of money is
the dream of a candle
smeared with fingerprints
the legible fingerprints
are a summons to
appear in court and
the court is a dream
of a well with no
bottom  .the well is the
dream of a single
coin falling off a cliff

## the stunned

the dream of the plate is the
dream of your hand was the
dream of coughing under the
table is the dream of the
sphere glowing in the
center of the table the
dream of the table is the
dream of the plate is the
dream describing the
death of your mother

## the backword

the dream of the translucent
lobster is the dream of a
translucent typewriter which
types all the words backwards
the sdrawkcab sdrow were the
dream of a bicycle parked
in a tree the tree is the
dream of a pencil
clicking its claws


## the coil

the dream of the pool of
water is the dream of
your eye focused on
the center of the earth
the dream of the earth is
the dream of the dream
of your breath of your
breathless inhalation
of the rain of frogs

## the snore

the dream of the net is
the dream of a poem
made of potato peelings
the dream of peelings is
the dream of the is it
the dream of the swallowed
the dream of the surface
seen from below the sur
face of the sea covered with plastic bottles

## the shoal

the dream of a seahorse is
the dream of an eraser
soaking in a cup of spit the
spit the dream of a light
bulb filling your mouth
your mouth the dream of
solid glass with something
moving inside it

## the knife

the dream of the kitchen is
the dream of legs lying
on a table the legs the
dream of apples sliced
in half and turning
brown the apples were
the dream of next week
when the laundry caught fire

## el pico

the dream of the stove is
the dream of the tunnel
that opens in the wall the
tunnel twists into dark
a pink stuffed bunny
stands at the entrance
the bunny is the dream
of your burning nose
stuffed with chiltepequines

## the chump

the dream of cooking rice
is the dream of frijoles
que te explican el sistema
oligareconómico los
frijoles are the dream
of your chest breaking wind
the breaking wind is the
dream of sausage
sewn to your hat like feathers

## los palitos

the dream of mezclar las
lentejas es el dream of
swimming en el mar el
mar es un dream of
cucumbers covered with
pepper la pimienta es el
sueño de la noche the
night the dream del día
que nace orondo in your
shorts

## la sopa seca

el sueño del movimiento per
petuo es el sueño de los
tallarines which lace your
shoes the shoes the dream
de las piedras esféricas que
hablan por horas y las
horas are the dream of a
flute which sounds like a
foghorn far up the coast


## el aperitivo

el sueño de cantar canciones
cursis fué el sueño de
olvidar tu nombre el sueño
de olvidarte el nombre es el
sueño de cantar canciones
cursis que son el sueño de

haberte olvidado el nOmbre

## el llamado

el sueño de estar en una
fiesta con amigos es el
sueño de una luz humeante
que vacila en el cielo raso
que es el sueño del cielo
vacío de estrellas es
el sueño de una rueda
que rueda al revés y que
rueda al revestido que
te espera en la calle oscura


## the spoon rest

el sueño de despedir a alguien
no es el sueño de tu mano
sino el sueño de tu mano
vestida con hierbas que
no es el sueño de la
torta bañada en salsa
sino el sueño de tu camisa
llevada al revés que no
es el sueño de la puerta
con su tecolote de plástico y
una rodaja enorme de queso

## the unit

the dream of tea is the
dream of a finger bound
with wire the wire the
dream of vapor rising
from your mouth and
the dream of a mountain
covered with green
hiding a band of
invisible guerrilla soldiers

## the neck

the dream of an apartment
is the dream of a box
floating in air is the
dream of ants chaining
up the walls the ants
were your dream of a
chocolate bar beaded
with moisture as the
morning fog clings
to your windows

## the bankers

the dream of your bed
was the dream of a sweaty
golf ball the ball the
dream of your dresses
packed in a box the box
the dream of your bed
full of golf balls and dr
esses was the dream of
folding money soaking in the sink


## el fin

the dream of the small house
is the dream of an absent
sidewalk the sidewalk might be
the dream of your finger sm
earing a bug on the window the
bug is not the dream or maybe
the dream of your sitting in a
chair unable to get up

## el rebozo

the dream of braids is the
dream of a ship casting
off the casting off is
the dream of birds returning
to land the birds your
dream of faucets open
and streaming air

## the shore

the dream of not being ready
is the dream of the death of
your friend the friend the
dream of your mind fluttering
in dark your mind the dream
of a tongue containing words
scribbled on chalchihuitl the
chalchihuitl a dream of the
book you explain your death in

## el pancho

the dream of ironing is the
dream of your butt un
folded across the kitchen
counter your butt will be the
dream of your mask in a bun
with catsup the catsup the
dream of heat rising up
your arm like a river

## el bostezo

el sueño del alba es el
sueño del albañil que se
dormita en la tina la
tina no será el sueño
de los libros de cordel
sino el sueño de tu
cara en una bolsa de
henequén la bolsa fué
el sueño olvidado del
sueño inútil de los
zapatos gastados

## the lobster

the dream of a pile of
shit was the dream
of a comb falling
to the floor the comb
was the dream of pants
twisted like rope the
pants a dream of the
hose whipping back
and forth which will
flush the shit down the stairs

## the shorn

the dream of the bathroom
with an open door is the
dream of a phone dropped
on the floor the phone the
dream of your hand holding
a key the key the dream of
having to pee the dream of
peeing is the dream of
waking up in a warm wet bed

## the fish

the dream of your children was
the dream of your lunchmeat
covered with hair it's the
dream of a doorway open to the
heat while the air conditioning
streams out the dream of the
heat is the dream of many
hands caressing your chest and
the dream of a motor
humming low in a basement

## la piedra del sol

the dream of the school principal
is the dream of forgetting the
dream of the circular calendar
the calendar's the dream of
yesterday happening tomorrow
and tomorrow's the dream of a
squirrel chewing a plastic bag
and speaking the language of Jiminy Cricket

## the husband

the dream of Devon is the
dream of a fountain which is
the dream of executive offices
full of hair the hair was the
dream of ice cream dripping
down the movie screen which
was the dream of swimming in a
pool with ice cubes and telephones


## el barking

the dream of riding in a
golf cart is the dream of a
clown with a basketball head
it's the dream of a flag hanging
limp in strong wind the wind's the
dream of retuning the voice
del spanglish clown asleep
said you tus eyes son
weendows revendadas

## la puerta

the dream del acensor es
el dream de paja scattered
inna wind es el sueño del
saber lo que es la nada
la nada's the dream of
blowing the ash off a
spoon the spoon's your
dream of sleep next to a
lime green goat in a party hat

## la cueva

the dream of selling aretes
is the dream of listening to
what the dog will say next
week the dog is the dream of
el pasaje bajo tierra con
Eleguá es el dream of a
door with your dirty shorts
behind it y un lápiz que
también es llave

## el aceituno

the dream of drinking a
gin martini is the dream of
your eyes your eyes the
dream of a nostril leaving
a trail on the laundry and a
trail which crosses the valley up
side down

## the corn

the dream of getting a
mammogram is the dream
of a plastic tube entering
your eye is the dream of a
lawn surrounding a huge
glass ball it's the dream of
the clouded faucet that
tells you it's time to
shave your legs

## el desayuno

el sueño de la plaza es
el sueño de un torbellino
de lenguas las lenguas
el sueño de la niebla
que sube del lago y el
lago ¡o lago! el sueño es
del ser nunca conocido
que conoces a fondo
como un plato de chilaquiles

## la lectura

the dream of the laptop
computer is the dream of a
large stone duct-taped to
your legs the stone was the
dream of the cold rising to
your waist and your waist
was the sandy sandwich or
the pages of a book smeared
with mayonnaise

## the lip service

the dream of your office at
work is the dream of light
flickering behind your
eyelids is the dream of a
giant tennis ball chewed by a
dog the ball a dream of your
empty lap which once held a
pencil

## the sleeve

the dream of the trip to France
will be the dream of laundry
falling from a plane the laundry
fills with wind the wind will be
your dream of a bookstore
where you buy lasagna the
lasagna the dream of water
rising to your chin

## the seal

the dream of listening to the
radio is the dream of
hamsters explaining your
dream the explanation's
the dream of yellow mustard
pooled in your hand your
hand is your cheek
dreaming of sitting in the
dark with crickets

## the reversal

the dream you won the
lottery is not a dream
but a jerking in your
stomach your stomach's a
dream of sudor y sombra
y el sudor the dream of fear
you'll win the lottery

## the interpretation

the dream of your mother-in-law
is the dream of finding your
place in the checkout line the
line is your dream of sleep in a
kitchen full of cigarette smoke the
smoke the dream of knowing
something certain but having
no idea what it is


## la niebla soñada

la niebla del sueño
es el lago de los ojos
el ruido del algodón
es el blanco del sueño
nomás las estrellas
que no duermen nunca
tienen esos sueños
apocalípticos de arena
nomás la arena
que no se despierta nunca
sueñan de la luz
que cae como lágrimas
del lago de los ojos

Ivan Argüelles Llorando con Bennett

## Ivan Argüelles hacks 3 Sueños

el bostezo macizo del mestizo
es el sueño del cíclope bigotudo
que duerme sobre las olas salgadas
de la cama de los sueños sin pelo
de la luna que desvaría locamente
dentro de su sueño de un barco
de piedra que vuela sobre el aire
de hieroglifos que por si mismos
son la escritura del sueño de la arena
cuyas orejas durmientes están llenas
del zigzageo de las abejas del sueño
de la isla sin alas que cae eternamente
por un cielo de ojos ciegos soñando
el bostezo macizo del mestizo
en su laberinto de llaves de tinta

Ivan Argïelles Eloqueciéndose detrás Bennett

## la boca soñada

el sueño de tu boca
es la boca de tu sueño
las dos cosas son el sueño
de la cuchara que vive
ardiendo en la boca
de tu sueño mientras
el sueño de tu cola
vive fumando dentro
el sueño de tu cuchara
yendo en circulos por
un cielo de sueños vacios
todo inexplicablemente
un sueño de tenedores
plásticos sin fin ay ay

Ivan Argüelles Detrás de las Inexplicaciones de Bennett

## fish dream

the dream of fish weaving through
electricity is the dream of lightning
wearing scales is the dream of Otto
Fischer learning to drive his dreams
right into the sand the dream is having

Ivan Argüelles Copping zzzs with Bennett

## el sueño de Tenochtitlan

el sueño de Xochimilco
es el sueño de las flores
flotando en su cama laberíntica
de agua y mercurio sueños
los dos de los niños perdidos
por el Parque de Chapultepec
en 1945 el año del sueño
de la luz metabólica del Presidente
Lázaro Cárdenas que todavía
dormita bajo la Avenida Insurgentes
con los sueños caóticos de la memoria
de los sueños negros de los
coches prefabricados del Norte
donde cantan los soñadores
apocalípticos de las tumbas
de todos los sueños de Moctezuma
antes de morirse en el sueño
del polvo que es un sueño
tan largo que ni se ven el tiempo
y su fin en ese sueño de Zochimilco
tan añorado y sin pies

Ivan Argüelles Siguiendo a Bennett

## the singer

the dream of a laptop computer
could be the dream of a pothole
full of mud and water but why
did the pothole have a face talking
to you in an incomprehensible
language? maybe the face is your
dream of the mar océano que
exhala un gas que entiendes?

## la ventana abierta

el sueño de tu cama ¿no es
el sueño de la calle espejeando
la luz lunar? ¿no es la luna
el sueño de tu cuchara per
dida en el río? y ¿no es el
río el sueño del diálogo que
sostienes con tu cara en la
ventana cerrada?

## "y los sueños sueños son"

the dream of jewelry is the
dream of your eyes which
are the dream of coins
pressed against your lids
but that would mean the
dream of eyes is the
dream of waking up in
your sleep which is the
dream of eating a
tasteless hamburger in a
nursing home full of mannequins




## the tongue

the dream of receiving a text
message is the dream of
a chinche mordiéndote la
axila es el sueño insondable
del silencio en un cubo de
piedras but the cubo de
piedras could never be
the dream of a text mess
age unless the message
were received upside down

## la boquita pintada

the dream of halloween is the
dream of a litro de mezcal
which was once the dream of
the dream of your face inside
out but then was the dream
of your tongue on a shiny
plate and the dream of a
tree losing all its leaves at
once but was that the
dream of you biting your
fingers raised to your mouth?

## the shoes

el sueño del parking es
el sueño o no es el sueño
de tus nalgas en una
tina de leche que no es
o es el sueño del timón
carbonizado en la parrilla
mas es o no es el sueño
de viajar en tren hacia
el norte donde hay
un río invisible

## the silt

the dream of being in a
car crash ought to be the
dream of your laundry
spread out on the bushes
to dry but it's the dream
of a belt won't hold up
your pants which is probably
the dream of a shopping cart
filled with bags of diapers

## the blue plate

the dream of the restaurant
would be the dream of a
pair of shoes if the rest
aurant  were a freezer
full of steaks which
would be the dream of a
cruise ship sinking to the
rocks below but it's the
dream of a car driving
upside down rolling
across the sky

## el orígen

el sueño de México es el
sueño del chilhuacle que te
cuenta la historia de la
piedra que guardas en el
bolsillo como talismán es el
sueño de una cueva de donde
sale un perro con plumas
de jaguar y es el sueño de
respirar el humo más
claro del mundo

## the answer

the dream of your Ex ,is it the
dream of your loud pocket ,the
dream of air swirling in your
mouth ,the dream of tunnels in
the back of your hand?  is it the
dream clouds disappearing in the
basement?  the dream of tuna
salad growing rancid in the fridge?

## the scissors

the dream of friends
was once the dream of
crumbs dancing on the table
but now is the dream of doors
opening and closing but still
still it's the dream of pillows
held under your arms so you
sleep standing up


## the dawn

the dream of coffee is the
dream of a car engine
rumbling in a cup of
motor oil the oil the
dream of your stream
of thought sliding down
the back of your neck

## the library

"the dream of the cigar
is just the dream of a cigar"

## the coils

the dream of a towel is the
dream of a chewed flag
falling from the mouth of a
bigot politician the politician
a dream of a shit sandwich
smiling like the face of
god ,was the face of god the
dream of washing your nose
and snoring on the steps
of the temple?

## la leche

el sueño de la música atonal
era el sueño del tonal que
cantaba tras la cerca de
tunas ,era el sueño del
silencio que te cantaba de
abejas y bonbones y quizá
el sueño era de las estrellas
que deletreaban tu nombre
en el cielo

## los libros

el sueño de enseñar es el
sueño de la muerte que
te espera en tu cama y al
mismo tiempo es el
sueño de despertar en un
cuarto desconocido donde
hay una garrafa de agua y una
silla hecha de huesos

## el efectivo

el sueño de estar en los
intersticios de una galaxia
es el sueño de estar con
amigos y el sueño de no
tener que hablar ni leer
que sería el sueño del
dinero transparente que
te dejas caer de las manos

## el podio

el sueño del cuerpo trans
parente es el sueño de una
pampa infinita donde sueñan
unos cangrejos del agua celestial
y es el sueño o el sueño de las
piedras sin peso que te esperan
dentro del televisor

## the soon

el sueño del artefacto en una
tierra desconocida es el sueño
insoñable de tu dedo índice
sangrando como manguera
quizá la manguera sea el sueño
de tu voz al explicar al revés
las palmeras de plástico tiesas
al borde de la carretera que
sale de un pecho que nunca has conocido


## el pulmón

el sueño del latir de un corazón
no puede ser el sueño de una
bicicleta oxidada en el mar
ni el sueño de la boca que
habla tostones de plátano macho
ni el sueño de la calavera de barro
ni tampoco el sueño del alfiler
de cristal que desaparece en tu
oreja hambrienta

## la leche soñada

la leche de la joyería
es el sueño de un texto
para analfabetos y todavía
las estrellas que comen
los rincones del espacio
son asmimismo el sueño
de la luna azteca cayendo
desde el zenit del azul
que es también el sueño
de un jaguar limpiando
sus patas en el agua del
sueño del espejo invisible
que está dormitando ahora
mismo en una hoja de acero
que sueña en el corazón
de un buey ciego atravesando
la montaña de sueños perdidos


Ivan Argüelles Inexplicablmente Siguiendo a Bennett

## "el alba"

el alba del café es la
taza del sueño que
se bebe despues de morir
a mediodía antes de
vivir a las tres de la tarde
pero la tarde del vaso
del alcohol puro es
la bebida de la oreja
que duerme dentro de
una hoja de mala hierba
pero ante todo el alba
del borracho es el sueño
mismo del dedo perdido
que sangra todavía en
el verde del alba gitana
de los romances viejos
cabidos en la otra oreja
la que queda detrás de
tanto sueño sin color
y sin dolor


Ivan Argüelles Dormitando al Pie de Bennett

## the cheese ball

the dream of the pier is the
dream of your tongue
entering the sandy canyon
the canyon's the dream of
your neck open to the
sea the sea's the dream
of an empty sports bar
with all the screens blazing
silent football games

## the bell mountain

the dream of the water slide is
the dream of closing your
eyes in a closet it's the
dream of jia wul wuhi the
devil's eye flickering in
the room beyond the room
is the dream of your
leg soaking in a bucket of pee

## the shining

the dream of a trophy is the
dream of a chewed leaf of
coca it's the dream of your
hat knowing it fell off
your hair your hair's the
dream of golden arms
melting in the morning sun

## in cempohualxochitl

the dream of investment is the
dream of glue-soaked dollars
in your pants and the dream
of a bloody stone stuck in
your hairdo your hairdo's the
dream of a dead bee
dancing around in a marigold

## the fall

the dream of stretching is a
dream forgotten in the bathroom
the bathroom was the dream
of a necklace crawling with
lice and the lice would be
the dream of the crown you
remembered if the stretching
were a dream of skirts
flapping on a line in the wind

## the shore face

the dream of bones is the
dream of your bed in a
cave high on a cliff where
the dream of femurs is the
dream of car exhaust
pooling in the garage and
the dream of a skull is the
dream of your favorite cat
sleeping on your face

## the fair

the dream of duct tape was
the dream of someone sh
outing in the bedroom it
was the dream of a sink
brimming with kool-aid and
a dream of a fork with
your tongue on its tines
the dream of your tongue
was the dream of rabbits
quivering in a nursing home
and the dream of a moon
glowing in the wet grasses
where your head once
lay dreaming of the
crow crawking at the
edge of the brillo pad competition

*JMB dreams a dream that is
not a dream of Bibiana Padilla Maltos*

## la primersa inexplicación

la primera inexplicación es
el sueño de Platón en su cueva
seguido por el sueño de una
lengua sin verbos en metamorfosis
con la cama que de veras es
un sueño sin piernas volando
como si fuera otro sueño
inexplicable de montañas con
alas ligeras como las plumas
de la seguna inexplicación ese
tumulto de sueños de caballos
verdes cazando las arenas del ojo
del ciclope soñando un mar
de huesos y aceites bajo un sol
de piedra todavia inexplicable
como los círculos de calor
en una tarde de oro español
cuando los sueños se derritan
en una nieve de sonidos sin color
que bajan poco a poca hacia
el sueño del relampago
zigzagueando por la ilusión
de una tercera inexplicación

Ivan Argüelles Volviéndose Loco con Bennett

## el sueño del grito

el sueño del grito no era
el grito del sueño sino
la niebla del sueño del
humo saliendo del sueño
del mar que yace muerto
bajo la cama de tu sueño
del dia sin tiempo afuera
del sueño que nunca era
sueño sino el humo de la
niebla del laberinto del sueño
de la luz que se pone al
fin del sueño del sol
cayendo como siempre del
sueño del infinito

Ivan Argüelles Perdido Dentro
del Sueño de Bennett

# BIBI'S DREAMS

## Bibiana Padilla Maltos

○

We were in a lounge bar, a group of unknown friends, my exhusband and his wife, and I. We were waiting for this artist to come join us from his concert. My exhusband had a huge white rat in his hands, almost the size of a car; he was carrying it like a baby and was amazed at how cute it was. He wanted to show me the "cutest teeth" he's ever seen. The rat was like any rat, but the nose was sticking out in a grape shape, like the old Mickey Mouse cartoons. I wanted nothing to do with that rat. He dropped it and ran away... The spot where the rat was dropped had something sticky with something moving in it, at first glance I thought they were cockroaches, but no: it was something furry, like hedgehogs but tiny and super furry.

○

In my dream, I was with an unknown person climbing up some staircase trying to get into this contemporary-style house by jumping in like felines. Once inside the house, we were to protect the people inside: a mom and a baby. I got under an open flight staircase and waited. The baby was playing with some red and yellow balls, the mom was peeking by the window. Outside, by the curve, next to the light post, there were three werewolves waiting for us and we were ready to attack, but, turns out they were only there to see if we were okay and pointed out a fallen pine and an open gate: they were seriously concerned about us. I woke up.

○

I had sparkles of dreams: walking around my house and seeing some dawn light on my son's room. I saw the kids coming into my bedroom playing and waking me up, wanting to turn the light on. I woke up.

○

In a short dream, there was a bar and a group of friends - and other unrecognizable people - were waiting for the rest of the group to arrive. We were to do some sort of guerrilla performances. We went outside the bar to greet someone at the parking lot, it was very cold and Jennifer Kosharek and I decided to go back inside. On our way back to the building, she talked about how we are so not used to the cold weather, as we went outside without our coats. We talked about the weather in California and Florida. We got confused and couldn't determine which one was the door for the bar, but did find it. Inside, Allen Bukoff was taking his coat off and greeting everyone with a hug.

○

I dream I was in a barn with all sorts of animals, this barn was just like any other but I didn't want to stay there. I went for a walk and after what seemed to be a very long walk I found myself in field full of trees; the more I was walking into the field the more my clothes were wearing out, as if the walking and the wind and the leaves' movement were tearing them and really beating my clothes. Then I started to look at the trees, they were apple trees but they where in all in different fruit shapes, some apples were falling down the tree and all of them were rolling and forming a pile by themselves.

○

In my dream we were receiving nuns that were leaving their habits behind but wanted to continue to work. The place was not really a clinic but a home. The nuns didn't like us to call them nuns or sisters because they had ran away from a convent and were really insisting we follow rules, and these rules were idiotic. There were blackboards on each wall and several nuns passing their chalk on them and erasing and numbering all these rules. They were making them as they pleased. Suddenly, they were the ones receiving people like you and me; they had taken over the place. The last person arriving told us that these nuns were cancer patients and by taking care of us were actually curing themselves. I woke up.

○

I dream that we were in the freeway looking for an interstate for which I couldn't remember all the digits. We were making jokes like "the exit is exactly where there is a gas station, a 7-eleven and a McDonalds" and laughing our loud that all exits were the same. We talked about how surreal it is in the United States and how in Mexico - and mostly EVERYWHERE - you must give an address, land marks plus any other specifics. I talked about how a GPS could never work, the street names change with the change of administration if not sooner... we realize THAT was more surreal than anything else. We exited, there was a gas station, a 7-eleven and a McDonalds, we rushed to see if they had a hose, but instead of washing ourselves, we buried our feet in the dirt.

○

In my dream I was really upset that my mom picked me up and was running errands and I really wanted her to go back and drop me off as I was going to be late. She was so stubborn. I found us going up a slope, I turned to the side and there was this school bus; in a blink of an eye I was riding that bus. When we got to the top of the slope we also got out of the bus. It was some sort of indigenous community; I turned around and told the group they were Cocopah natives and how they made pectoral necklaces in this and that way; next thing you know we are about to eat dinner and they were serving food over a worm. The food wasn't good but a rounded warm rye bread was the best thing I've ever ate. I realized we were in a CULT. I tried to find acquaintances, or my mom, or someone and nothing... I followed these girls; I could hear them talking but could not understand them: cult slang.

O

I don't recall the entire dream, I abruptly woke up and cannot seem to snatch all the pieces floating in my head, but, in my dream we were getting together to go somewhere to perform with our ukuleles; it was messy but there were chairs, a lot of music stands with their music sheets; I was concerned once more about being cold. By the time I made it to my "spot" my two jackets were gone. Someone pointed that one of them was on display to be sold; I got closer to take a look but that was not my jacket and I explained my jacket was not a woman's jacket, it was a marlboro suede jacket (which I had in real life), one that my mom gave my dad as her first present and one I kept for many many years.

O

I dream I was at home, in Mexico. The son of my boss was there along with other coworkers; we were working there because we didn't have an office in Mexico. We had very old computers and there were cables EVERYWHERE. My mom had made this specialty pastry for my coworkers. I offered them some but nobody was liking this creamy mint they were filled with.

○

Growing up at the border - and where the San Andres fault is located - crossing the border and having earthquakes are a recurrent dream. One of my recent border dreams has been that I am in my car, waiting in line and I realize I don't have my passport or someone who is traveling with me does not have their passport. Most people don't know but, once you are in the line to cross there is no way back nor out. So, here I am, sitting in my car, thinking what am I going to tell the customs dudes, hoping it is not a woman, women are way much more strict. I get to the booth and they ask about the passport, what we were doing in Mexico, what movies we have watched; they sent us to second inspection.... at second inspection we are waiting in this room to be called, only it is no longer the american but the mexican side. We walk out and see a bank robbery which we are able to stop with our kung fu kicks.

○

I dream I needed to take a break and was walking with one of my university's colleagues toward her car, a burgundy Oldsmobile. We drove around trying to find a place to eat, but most streets were closed. We could see some smoke coming out of a driveway. There was a private community that had rocks in flames and they were lining up these fired up rocks in this trail. We couldn't see, but we knew they were trying to get people in there to do something "bad" with them.

○

I dream I was on Facebook creating an invitation for an event, the event was going to take place in New York City and I wanted to invite Mark Bloch. I could not find him on the event page. I could not find him on my list of friends. I could see he was on Facebook but we were no longer friends, he had unfriended me. I felt really sad. I didn't know what did I do to be unfriended.

**○**

I dream we were in some sort of gold carts that became some sort of tricycle skateboards operated electrically. We were going back and forth from a station to some sort of hardware store. I needed to order some floor finishing, but not any particular floor... I explained to the attendant that I needed something to cover my cement floor, I had already painted in a certain way and I needed some transparent polymer to cover the surface; it also needed to have some sparkles mixed in, but not too many. I waited for the mix to be done and it was put in some sort of vacuum because it needed constant movement; this vacuum had a huge pump and, by activating it you'd get X amount of glitter in it. The guy regulated the size of the glitter particles I wanted and I explained to him I only wanted ONE pump. With a lot of difficulty, he pushed the pump and I could see how the glitter got into the polymer that kept rotating... I thought "my floors are going to kick ass!". I woke up.

**○**

I dream Keith Buchholz didn't have a place for the next Fluxfest so I offered my home; only my home was not the current one but the one were I lived as a child. Everything was there, the long corridors, the glass doors, etc. People had already taken some of the bedrooms. Reed Altemus and I were sharing mine, which had that old console with a TV. Allen Bukoff took the master bedroom. C. Mehrl and John M. Bennett had the room between those two, some people were taking the living room, the den, and so on. A lot of people were arriving, people that I knew from the group and people who I didn't know, and audience, etc.; I directed them to the backyard. I was shocked to see two of my friends taking a nap, naked; I realized one of them had just cheated and was unsure if I should say something. The doorbell rang, it was a delivery for tables, chairs and table cloths, I asked them to go around by the alley. The doorbell rang again, it was the musicians, I directed them to the alley entrance. I was weirded out by these deliveries but I figured someone was performing something with this. I went outside and discovered there was obviously a party going on with the "audience" and all those unknown people, with caterers and waiters everything. In the game room, my friends were gathered in a circle, taking turns to perform with very little light.

⬤

I dream I was in a library/gallery because I was co-curating a show. The library entrance was very, very busy. I was ordering a coffee and a snack and needed to wait for the other curator. Sitting on a bench, people watching and trying to remember if all the artwork arrived, what was the space, all the things that I may need for mounting and how kissing may not be cheating, but it was, so I was feeling depressed and wanted to quit the show.

⬤

I dream I was at that yellow house we rented after ours burned down when I was a kid. I wasn't living there but visiting my mom. I got out of the car and I realized in front of the house was a medical office, with a roller head metal door on the side. I saw a delivery guy and a doctor acting shady. I opened the patio gate and was trying to lock it behind me, as quick as I could, because the doctor and his helpers where crossing the street in my direction. I turned the key once. I turned the key twice. I turned once again and it broke leaving the top of the key between my thumb and my index fingers. I thought, I cannot believe these new keys made of a mix of paste and metal. I took the next key and was going to put it in the door keyhole when the doctor was right by the fence, saying he's been keeping an eye on us. My sister opened the door and I felt relieved. Inside the house, things were like they used to be while living there. All rooms were exactly the same. That house was a bit labyrinthine, when I finally found my mom, she was with my other sister; her body was covered with folded orange towels, she even had a smaller one on her forehead. She was just there, lying down. My sister was in shock, she looked at me and started to cry, said my mom was dead.

I approached them and asked "is this it? is this how it actually is?" and picked up one of her arms. My mom started breathing and removed the orange towel from her forehead. I thought "wait a minute, how can this be?". I woke up.

**o**

I dream that I needed to get ready for work. I picked up my clothes and went into the bathroom to take a shower. The bathroom was my current bathroom, only it had a lot of sunlight and I realize I didn't really need to turn on the lights. I jumped into the shower and it no longer was squared; it was twice its size in a rectangle with transparent panels. I thought of the need to wipe the panels after each shower so the water wouldn't leave marks. I stepped out of the shower and one of the walls was torn down linking this bathroom with the next, I had no idea why the fuck we would have done that, what were we thinking? I woke up, then fell asleep again.

○

In my next dream I made it to work with the clothes I
previously picked. I did some errands in the office and came
downstairs. This lobby was very similar to the dream days
ago about the library. It was some sort of rounded building
and this lobby had a cafeteria and a gift shop. I sat down on
a cement bench against a wall with an unknown acquain-
tance, for some reason I needed to make him feel better
and we needed to talk. I put my tray on my spot and walked
over to the gift shop. I was looking for some book and on
the shelf a book grabbed my attention, I took it and it was a
book about my ex husband's work, not essays, not short
stories, not a novel, but what he always wanted to do,
cinema. I felt good for him. I woke up.

○

I dream I was at work and I had a present at my desk that
needed a bow. The box was stuck to itself and I was trying to
fix it, but, by fixing it it was starting to look beat-up. A
coworker came in and wanted to see what the present was
and who it was for... I didn't want to disclose either thing.
Later on, Dr. House (from the TV series) came to give me a
spin, I was in a wheelchair. He took me through the parking
lot, all the way to the end of the building and back, making
wheelies and making fun of it all.

○

I dream I was at my kids' school, they were having some sort
of celebration, like the end of year art show or something.
Since this was the very last day of classes we were allowed to
pick up from the walls any art or photos of our kids... I took
down all the ones I saw and noticed that by the corner were
a couple of tables together with some hay. The closer I got
the more detailed it was. They had some Ginny Lloyd

books and it was almost an altar to her, with some mailart made by the kids in collaboration with her, it didn't make sense, so I woke up.

**O**

I dream I was driving up a mountain in reverse and only guided by the rear view  mirrors. Once we got to the top of the mountain I decided to switch seats with my copilot to be able to drive facing forward (yes, apparently the steering wheel was switchable). While driving down the mountain and into the town we were going to, I noticed the road made of stone, I noticed that even though there were  no lights I could see the island next to the town, and the waves and the clear water... it was a beautiful night. We parked, we walked into the restaurant to meet our party which was my folks and brothers, which it was odd because they weren't the ones in my real life, but I hugged them and kissed them; it seems I was Fernando Llanos, because my copilot became his wife Jessica Herreman and she was happy to meet my "family". It didn't make sense, so I obviously woke up.

**O**

Soñé que tocaban la puerta, que la abría y que no era nadie; al volverla a cerrar, el gabinete de los cubiertos se abría y uno a uno los cuchillos, los tenedores y las cucharas se acomodaban en la mesa del comedor. Así mismo, los distintos platos, las servilletas. Al caminar a la cocina me percaté que estaba alguien limpiándose las botas llenas de lodo, en la entrada al patio trasero. No puse mucha atención solamente pregunté "¿y tienes hambre?", sí, me respondió. Como no encontré el cucharón para el caldo, puse la olla de barro sobre un protector en la mesa y me regresé a terminar de calentar las tortillas de maíz... "quiero una de harina", me dijo... la calenté y la puse en el tortillero... Cual fue mi sorpresa que al sentarme a la mesa ya estaba todo dispuesto, y la llorona me estaba esperando, para contarme de los árboles que había plantado, pero sobre todo, de las otras cosas que también había enterrado. Y desperté.

●

Soñé que estaba en otra ciudad, una ciudad pintoresca, en un festival de arte. Estaba en la suite de un hotel que había sido intervenida con un tragaluz muy particular de Daniel Ruanova. En mi sueño, recordé que la fachada del hotel era demasiado conservadora e inmediatamente corrí a la calle con mi cámara para tomar una foto del pico saliendo de mi habitación... Al llegar al lado del hotel donde se encontraba dicha instalación, había mesas y gente tomando café sobre la banqueta... tomé las fotos y pedí un café. Y desperté.

●

I dream I was in my current home. There were some muddy puddles in my backyard and some of the blocks of the back wall were taken down leaving a big hole in it. The back neighbors were coming into my backyard but at that point the backyard was the one were I grew up. I went out there and they told me they were having a party and needed to refrigerate some food items. I went to a VERY BIG ASS refrigerator we had and threw out a couple of things that were no longer good. The refrigerator was pretty much empty. I woke up.

●

I went back to sleep and I dream I was at the kindergarten dropping or picking up my kids - it was unclear at the time. Then I realize I just had drop them off and came back for something. I was IRRITATED big time because I had just dropped them off and the teacher was putting them to sleep.

I was yelling, angry, telling her my kids didn't sleep that early and questioning why did she do that, AND HOW!? did she drug them!? The teachers started to laugh at me and I stormed to the front office to talk to the director, when I asked myself why would I let them laugh at me and I woke up.

○

I dream we were living back in Seal Beach and we were joining the annual bike ride, but only to this particular restaurant / bar. This time we needed to wear pajamas and Devon brought these transparent ones that he put over his clothes. I told him that the point of the pajamas was to just wear them, and they didn't go over the clothes. We rode our bikes by ourselves without the group, barefooted and in our pajamas. I could feel the edges of the pedals on my bare feet.

○

We got to the complex (which doesn't really exist in Seal Beach) and something happened, almost like I skipped part of the dream, because I was sitting on a movie theater and the movie was ending, I was sitting by myself, enjoying my popcorn and my soda and reading the credits. I walked out of the theater and knew I needed to catch up with Devon at the bar. I jumped over a cabled fence and continued to walk, barefoot and now in a long summer dress... I walked by the pool on the cement floor, the floor was colored red and green. I saw my friend Cynthia, a colleague from the university, we sat on the equipales by the pool and she told me she was getting married in September (in my dream it was this current month, July). And, as always, I started questioning if I would be able to make it to her wedding with this short notice and all the way to Spain and I woke up.

●

I dream I was having cramps. I gathered all my clothes and went into my childhood dressing / bathroom. Everything was the same, in a greenish color; I turned the shower on and while getting into the water I realized some blood clots were getting stuck in the drain.

●

My dream seemed to fast forward to find myself riding a moppet with one of my childhood friends, Jorge. He kissed my cheek and I woke up.

●

I dream I was sitting in the family room and Devon said our daughter was outside playing. I asked how was she going to come back inside and felt anxious that she was outside unsupervised. He explained he left the garage door open for her. I went into the garage and saw the door open, and it was dark outside. I walked to the curb and didn't see anyone on the street. I ran inside and told Devon she wasn't there; we both ran down the street yelling her name.... We saw a big bouncy house in the corner of the next block, a lot of kids jumping in it. As we approach the corner we saw our daughter on the street running to get to the curb while a very fast sport car passed by. The driver cut us off and parked in the apartment complex next to us, I told him he was an asshole and he replied in a foreign accent "yes, I am, so what?". We got to the bouncy house and picked up our daughter. While I was carrying her on the way home, I started to question why was the bouncy house there? how did she get all the way there? and, as every time I question my dreams, I woke up.

○

I dream I was in some sort of field, but doing production line work with romaine lettuce. The field was surrounded by mountains and fresh air, and it seems like I was loving my work there, it was very early in the morning and I could see the sun about to rise. I needed to line up three heads of lettuce and cut the bottom portion of it to make them even, then pass it on to the next person to maybe bag it, or something. There was a supervisor talking to us, workers, and saying how so and so had chosen a different schedule. There was a woman saying she wanted to start at 1 AM and I was thinking to my self "now that is early"; the supervisor told her he couldn't do that because she had a baby and how he would hate it to be the reason for an unattended child. While they were talking, I walked to the edge of that area and realized there was another field, a broccoli field; but the broccoli was growing as small bushes, like two feet tall, then people would cut them down to the size we know. I went back to my line and we were now packaging roasted chicken breasts; I was in charge to line them up in a foam tray and take some of the fat out, then pass it to be wrapped with plastic. I thought, what does cooked chicken have to do with a field of vegetables? I obviously woke up, like I always do when I question my dreams.

○

(Last night I went out with an all-time friend and his coworker, we went to a bar in Long Beach. The music was not like I remembered, but I still had fun and had some well-deserved drinks. At the end of the night, they walked me to my car and said goodbye).

In my dream, I repeated what just happened last night: I arrived at the restaurant-bar and walked up the stairs to the roof tap to meet Jorge and his coworker Arturo. I sat at their table and drank my drinks, and it was like either I passed out at the table or I simply had a black out. I remember things coming back to me and the waiters and waitresses were telling us they were closing. I thought, how did this happen? It was like a time slip and I think I didn't wake up only because I turned around and my jacket was not there, so I was obviously worried about that. I look to see if my purse was at the bench, and it was. I opened it and my billfold was there, everything was there, but my jacket. I was rushing to leave and kinda scanning the place for my jacket, I saw one, but it wasn't mine. Finally, jacket in hand, I walked outside only to find my friends getting into their car, brought by the valet. I thought, what the fuck!? they didn't even say good night! I started walking towards the garage where my car was parked. It was late and dark and people were lying on the curb trying to sleep, or playing music, or smoking. I asked what time it was and heard someone say it was midnight. Two acquaintances were walking along with me, apparently they lived close by. I remembered the garage closed at midnight and said how am I going to get home!? and if I leave the car there, how will I manage in the morning!? One of the acquaintances said he'd give me a ride, but, when we reached the corner we saw a woman opening the garage door. I ran there and asked if she could please let me take my car, she didn't want to, at first, but the guy that was going to give me a ride convinced her, I got in my car and left. I didn't wake up, but do not remember what was next.

●

I dream I was heating some leftovers, but I couldn't really see what they were, it was a mixture of things; but I was seriously working on that stove and skillet.

Later on, I was talking to a friend while dressing up, putting on some high heels, a dress and we were ready to go... I was driving in my home town, on Reforma Avenue, it was supposed to be night time, although it was very illuminated, with some dust... almost like gunpowder, even if it didn't smell like it.

○

Una camada de gatos hizo que frenara mi carro de golpe; y una parvada de pájaros (sí, en la noche) clareó el polvo frente a mí.

○

Soñé que teníamos en casa un Jacuzzi. Estaba esperando a unos amigos y mientras estaba al teléfono con mi mejor amigo, Carlos. La conversación fue eterna; hablamos por muchísimo tiempo, de cosas triviales, de cosas de más importancia, y finalmente dijo que seguía en el DF y que no iría a mi casa. Al momento de terminar la llamada, un grupo de paipais entró a mi casa y rodeando el jacuzzi cantaron una canción.

○

I dream I was in the bathroom of my childhood home and in the middle of it there was some sort of glass cover over a pedestal. There was nothing inside and I was intrigued about why would that be there. I finished getting ready, walked outside and joined a family reunion we were having in the backyard. There were tables beautifully arranged. Behind the backyard there was no longer the alley, there was a canal now, and we were looking for a map to see where did the canal go and if we could navigate it.

○

I dream Luc Fierens was having a poesia visiva show in Los Angeles and I was trying to reach out to him to ask if he was coming or just sending his work. Allen Bukoff (why am I always dreaming of him!?) knocks on our door to tell us Luc called him and was flying to California. We sat down and started organizing a welcome gathering for him and were talking about where would everyone be sleeping. I was concerned about his cats, but Allen built some sort of cubbies for them under the bed Luc would use.

Next thing in my dream I was getting into the car and driving to the airport, I drove into the parking spots and woke up.

○

Soñé que estaba revisando una computadora, quería asegurarme de que algo sucediera pero no estaba segura de qué era exactamente lo que estaba buscando o esperando. Estaba de visita en una casa que no sé de quién era, pero, al estar en la computadora me di cuenta de que mi mamá estaba viviendo con "ellos". Mi mamá me encaminaba a las habitaciones que estaba ocupando, era una especie de casa para invitados. Ya dentro de la casa, me decía que estaba estudiando un libro que era el mismo que yo traía en mi bolso. Le enseñé cómo lo tenía marcado con un plumón amarillo fluorescente. Cuando quise voltear el libro para ver el título, desperté.

○

Soñé que estaba en la oficina, pero no puedo recordar por qué o para qué.

Lo siguiente en mi sueño fue estar en un den, acostada en el piso, con otra persona y cubriéndonos con una cobija;

180

estábamos a punto de ver una película y nos preguntábamos quién tenía el control de la televisión, cuado caímos en cuenta que lo tenía un amigo que estaba recostado en el sillón.

Luego, no sé cómo fui a dar a una explanada, en alguna escuela de meditación. En dicha escuela tenían varios métodos para meditar y yo quería entender cómo era que funcionaba una especie de péndulo que estaba en un recuadro de fina arena como de 10x10 metros: había que tomar cerca de una pared dicho péndulo, caminar hacia una esquina y soltarlo, pero estaban otras personas pisando la arena y me era imposible comenzar mi "meditación". Como no se movían y seguían pasando otras personas y no se daban cuenta que estaban interrumpiendo, decidí irme a sentar al zacate con mi hermana Roxana, quien estaba haciendo unos letreros que tenían que ver con una solicitud de trabajo. Me di cuenta que había puesto al final México y un número telefónico americano, fue cuando le dije que debía borrar la palabra México y simplemente dejar el número americano. En lugar de borrarlo quiso tacharlo haciendo otro tipo de letras sobre la palabra y yo, con un corrector líquido lo corregí.

○

Soñé que estaba en una reunión en casa de un excompañero de la escuela y estaban haciendo Rusos Blancos de una manera muy extraña: sin Kahlúa y sin vodka; estaba tratando de averiguar cómo era esto posible pero me sentí muy cansada, y salí a sentarme en una silla hecha con yute, remojando mis pies en el agua de la alberca. De pronto hizo viento, y el viento trajo hojas secas, muchas, que cubrieron toda el agua de la alberca. Desperté.

○

Soñé que estaba caminando en un desierto, hacia una especie de oasis, la arena comenzó a concretarse en unos bloques, y estos bloques a su vez comenzaron a despegarse uno del otro, flotando sobre agua. Me quité los zapatos y remangué mis pantalones para no salpicarme de agua. Al final del camino estaban papi y mami (mis bisabuelos) y Devon. Recordé que papi y mami murieron hace tiempo y que Devon y yo estamos vivos, y pensé que nada de esto tenía sentido. Desperté.

○

I dream I was in my grandparents' game room and I was there because we needed to clean up some boxes that were being kept there. While moving a box we noticed there was a mouse, and then another, they were running around like crazy; we opened a closet and these mice had fur, a lot of it. We were able to take a couple out, and they grew to the size of a CAT, their faces were flattened, like pugs. I turned to my right and there was a papier maché devil that was moving, I thought there were mice under him, but, the devil flexed to lay an egg. The egg was the size of an ostrich's, it was yellow and it was soft and slippery. I woke up.

○

Soñé que estaba en una clase que no sabía exactamente de qué era; la instructora estaba haciendo unos ejercicios de estiramiento al final de ésta (que fue cuando mi sueño comenzó, o al menos es ese el momento en que lo comencé a recordar); la instructora estaba en el suelo, estirándose y explicándole a la gente por qué era importante estirar los músculos e interrumpió la explicación para ponerse a platicar con otro instructor. Una persona del grupo le dijo que por favor atendiera la clase y por fin finalizamos. En lo que la gente agarraba sus bolsas y equipo, la instructora explica que quiere que los que tengamos aptitudes de baile regresemos con nuestras hojas coreográficas. Me acerco y le pido que anote mi nombre, me pregunta dónde estudié y qué tipo de danza.

Salí de este estudio y me puse a caminar yendo a casa, crucé la calle antes de llegar a la esquina y una señora con acento argentino comenzó a ofenderme, diciéndome que por qué tenía yo que cruzar la calle así, que yo era el tipo de persona que todos odiaban y un sin fin de insultos, volteé y le dije que parara pero seguía insultándome; entonces se me ocurrió meter la mano a mi bolso y pretender que iba a sacar una pistola. La señora comenzó a gritar que no me iba a atrever a sacar una pistola cerca de la escuela, pero yo hice como si le apuntara la pistola dentro de mi bolso, alzándolo. Me apresuré y entré a la escuela para cortar camino, la señora entró después y yo pensé que estaba siguiéndome, pero había entrado a la explanada de la escuela porque le había una ceremonia para los abuelos (ella era una de las abuelas de los niños de la escuela). Salí por la reja del lado opuesto y me metí al primer negocio que ví; era como un establo urbano en el que tenían ponies y cabras, ambos del mismo color, como dorado. Pregunté cuánto costaban, setenta y cinco dólares, dijo el muchacho. Me pregunté qué estaban haciendo los ponies con las cabras. Desperté.

**O**

Soñé que estaba en una casa con muchas habitaciones, muchas puertas y muchas escaleras. Estaba mi prima Ilse con sus hijos, quienes estaban jugando con los míos. Varios familiares se fueron al Valle de Guadalupe, a la fiesta de la vendimia, y yo estaba muy molesta porque nadie me dijo que iban a ir. Estábamos tumbados sobre unos arbustos de arándano con otro amigo, René Castillo quien había traído unos saladitos dulces (esas ciruelas secas); de ahí nos fuimos a una exposición en la que iba a dar una plática... saludé a algunos de los que atendieron la conferencia en los pasillos... estaba un poco oscuro; entré a la tienda de regalos a buscar un vestido bordado, pero, me dí cuenta que costaba tres mil pesos y yo solamente llevaba mil. Desperté.

●

Soñé que estaba en casa de mi hermana Luciana y estaba una señora limpiando su casa. La señora me pedía que si le podía leer un mensaje que mi mamá le había dejado junto con un dinero (aparentemente no sabía leer). Le leía el mensaje y el mensaje tenía algunos errores ortográficos, le dí el dinero a la señora. El mensaje era una indicación para que la señora se tomara un medicamento. Había también, en un platón, unas piezas de pollo empanizadas. Comí un poco y desperté.

●

I dream I was at my current job, it was Christmas season and my boss had died. His son was taking over the company but as expected, he had no clue how to do things. He had called all the office employees to come over and get a Christmas bonus. Instead of handing a check to each one, he had made a tower of cash alternating the direction of each stack of money for whichever employee, then dividing it with a plate facing down. I was impressed that the money wasn't falling, and was also impressed how he was handling the situation: he was asking each employee on the line to come forward and take one stack of bills, and that was the Christmas bonus for that particular person. The bills could be anywhere from one dollar up to a hundred, they could be mixed, it was all a game.

○

I dream there was this creature that was some type of
lobster, and it was fading to the point of a translucent
lobster. Someone had placed it inside a pool, we couldn't
take her out, we finally took a cleaning net and we pulled
out something that was moving but that we couldn't see
except for the swirls of water when it did move. It was not
the lobster but a seahorse that was growing. In its cheek he
had a mark, and inside the mark was the name of its species,
what it was, where it came from and who was the owner.
Supposedly we were to give it to someone as a token of
friendship.

○

No sé qué fue exactamente lo que soñé, pero era una
secuencia tipo "stop motion" en la que me encontraba en
una cocina, y en la estufa de la misma había diferentes ollas,
en cada una había distintos tipos de arroz. Yo tomaba un
tazón enorme en la que ponía una cucharada de cada arroz,
lo mezclaba con dos palitas de bambú y lo pasaba a los
comenzales. Y tomaba otro tazón y a seguir mezclando y
sirviendo.

○

Soñé que estaba en una fiesta hablando con amigas que no
conocía sobre tipos de té, de la soledad, del temor de estar
solas... les pedía sus números telefónicos y al despedirme,
me dicen que tenían una enfermedad, pero no podía
entenderles el nombre y comencé a copiarlas, finalmente
me pude ir y al salir me di la vuelta para hacer un ademán
de adiós a los que no me pude despedir y me di cuenta que
estaban disfrazados.... llegué a mi departamento cantando
canciones cursis y me acosté en una cama pequeña, como
para niños.

○

I dream we were living in a smaller house, almost like
a cabin. I was braiding my hair and running upstairs to get
ready for some wedding. It was early in the morning and the
sun was not even out. Devon was taking an ironing board
out for me to iron a shirt and the kids were waking up.

○

I dream I was in a movie theater and I needed to go back to
my seat, I took the elevator and it was the wrong one.
Once "the people" noticed I was getting into the private
offices they switched the elevator to eject me into a fountain.
From there I took a golf cart to go home. While at home,
Devon and I were getting ready to give an open house
because we were selling the house. The realtor arrived and
checked the house first, then said it was going to be a
success... a bunch of people arrived, mostly people who
spoke broken spanish. I was weirded out about the whole
situation and asked Devon to leave; we took off walking and
there was some sort of plaza, we approach a food truck to
get absinthe and off I went to get a mammogram.

○

I dream I was buying a laptop at and for work, then left the
office to attend a party and meet Devon there. I drove side
streets while listening to the radio. At the party, there were a
lot of people, and I was told we (my mother-in-law and I)
had just won a trip to France. I was excited for the trip but
unsure how it would go with my mom-in-law. I woke up.

○

Soñé que me estaba terminando de arreglar, sentada en mi
cama, poniéndome aretes en las orejas y demás bisutería.
Luego, mandando un mensaje de texto a Karim, para ver si

186

nos íbamos a ver en Seal Beach. Era Halloween y la gente ya traía puestos sus disfraces y ya iba camino de bar en bar. Yo me quedé estacionada en la esquina del banco; había un carro mal estacionado, bloqueando la calle principal y otro carro al dar la vuelta se le estampó, chocando también contra el mío y reventando las micas de la parte trasera. Al bajarme, la conductora se estaba haciendo la loca... al llegar la policía pedimos que hiciera rápidamente la multa de tránsito y desperté.

●

I dream I was at a restaurant in Mexico City sitting by a square table with Alejandro (my exhusband), Martín Solares, David Miklos and Carlos Gutiérrez (my best friend)... We were having this "writers meeting" because something was about to be published under our names. I was trying to zone out of the conversation Alejandro was making, because we all knew each other and it seemed way too solemn for this meeting. Martín rushed me to finish my coffee, he flipped the cup and we waited. David lit a cigar saying he had just started this habit. Carlos was making fun of us all and was telling us stories that were giving us some serious and loud laughs. It was time: Martín flipped back the cup and decided not to read it, said it was "too intense". A photographer from Tijuana, Josué Castro, passed by and said hi, said he was in a photo shoot with the chefs of that restaurant (it was almost like a "dream ad"). I asked David to pass the cigar and was unsure of what I was going to do. The cigar was falling apart, it had one of its leaves unrolled and hanging 6 inches from the cigar. I rolled it and gave it a try while making fun of him not knowing how to smoke. The waitress came by and told us we couldn't smoke inside the restaurant while asking us to take turns to do so in the patio. We all stood up and walked towards the patio, but the patio was so small we realized why the waitress had asked us to do it one by one. We came back to our table to take our places. We had our bags, books, yellow notebooks, etc. David's notebook had some drawings his daughter Ana did. There was also a wooden bucket in the center of the table. I took a towel that was soaking inside of it, extending it and showing two big wholes on it, and saying "¡mira David, nuestras perras!". I woke up.

○

Me soñé explicando la música microtonal. Así. Con una terminología que ni yo lograba comprender.... comencé explicando variaciones de tonos e intervalos, que bueno, eso es lo que primero que se me vino a la mente, pero después, continué hablando de tiempos y espacios y de pronto, me ví elevándome en el pódium en el que estaba rodeda de una galaxia, ibamos 3 personas como abalanzándonos para poder llegar a una especie de estación. Ví a una persona - o ente - que se quedaba sin oxígeno, ví su cuerpo flotar y sus pupilas dilatarse. Ví, también, su corazón con latidos juntos y espaciados. La tomé entre mis brazos y me puse a pensar cómo fue que la vi dentro de su artefacto, cómo fue que ví sus pupilas dilatarse tanto (casi de forma caricaturesca) si tenía los párpados cerrados.... me pregunté cómo fue que ví la luz emanar de su cuerpo y ví los latidos de su corazón.. y desperté.

○

I dream I was at the end of the pier and a very big guy was making the pier sink, as if it were elastic, we had part of our bodies inside the water; I could see an old VW spinning (as they were impermeable) and I kept yelling at him he needed to shut the windows close or he would sink.... I saw the big guy sliding on the water toward me, he had a trophy in his hands for first place of who-knows-what-sort of competition;

next, there was a family of ladies and their kids sliding towards the end collapsing with the third place trophy winner.... we walked towards the beginning of the pier, towards an open plaza. I took a ball of cheese snacks and started to look where to sit... I finally found my table, a tall cocktail bar table; there was a girl sitting there and more people started to come and join us. There were some bags at the table and we were passing them around. A guy ended up approaching us and letting us know he was so happy we were able to make it and that we would finally be able to talk about the investment in the new school acquisition we just made. I stretched and I could feel my hip bones while listening to the lady next to me say out loud "never in this life would I have thought I would end up investing in a school" and I replied "Y yo juré no volver a poner un pie en escuela alguna". I woke up.

## CODA

Bibi:
aving their habits behind but wanted to continue to work. The place was not really a clinic but a home. The nuns didn't like us to call them nuns or sisters because they had ran aw

JMB:
e ream o he abits ind ut ant o tin o ork. he ace as no rea a clin ut a om. he uns id ik u o all hem uns o ist beca hey ha an a

!!

# NOTES